C000069051

A KICK IN ＿ＪＢＬＥＳ

A KICK IN THE BAUBLES

by Gordon Steel

JOSEF WEINBERGER PLAYS

LONDON

A KICK IN THE BAUBLES
First published in 2007
by Josef Weinberger Ltd
12-14 Mortimer Street, London, W1T 3JJ
www.josef-weinberger.com
general.info@jwmail.co.uk

ISBN 978 0 85676 294 9

Printed in England by Biddles Ltd, King's Lynn, Norfolk

For Glenda, and the Christmases we have spent together

A KICK IN THE BAUBLES was first produced by Hull Truck Theatre Company (John Godber, Artistic Director) at the Hull Truck Theatre, Hull on 16th December 2005 with the following cast:

FRANK	Robert Hudson
JEAN	Jackie Lye
HARRY	Jason Furnival
DOREEN	Christine Cox
GARY / DARREN	Chris Connel
JULIE / ALEX / MILLY	Natalie Blades

Directed by Gareth Tudor Price

Designed by Pip Leckenby

Lighting designed by Graham Kirk

CHARACTERS

FRANK

JEAN

HARRY

DOREEN

GARY

JULIE

ALEX

MILLY

DARREN

THE SET

The set is dominated by Christmas colours and is framed with a dark blue sky and silver snowflakes that bleed into the reality of the family home. It consists of a living room with a small section of a kitchen up right and a door up left of centre that leads into a passage which in turn leads to upstairs, the dining room and the front door. A door up right leads into the kitchen. It is assumed that the back door is through the kitchen, off right (GARY and JULIE frequently use the back door and enter into the living room through the kitchen).

Left of the upstage door is a window and beneath the window is a small dining table with a couple of chairs. Through the window we see sections of privet. A Christmas tree is up centre, to the right of the upstage door, and to the right of that is a sideboard. The living room is filled with a three-piece suite: the settee is centre with a chair to the right and left of it. The chair to the right is regarded as HARRY's chair and to the right of that is a small table. The coffee table sits centre, in front of the settee. A Hi-Fi is situated up right behind HARRY's chair next to the kitchen door. The sideboard, walls and doors are adorned with Christmas cards.

ACT ONE

Scene One

Christmas Eve. 7.15 AM. A living room. FRANK *enters carrying two Asda carrier bags.*

FRANK   (*to the audience*) I bloody hate Christmas.

                (JEAN *enters laden with carrier bags.*)

JEAN   Are you sure you can manage?

FRANK   You've bought too much.

JEAN   I don't want you hurting yourself.

FRANK   Where the hell are we gonna put this lot?

JEAN   I don't want you putting your back out.

FRANK   That fridge is chock-a-block.

JEAN   You have a sit down, take the weight off your wallet.

FRANK   Where the hell's it all gonna go?

JEAN   I know where I'm gonna shove it if you don't stop complaining.

                (JEAN *trudges off to the kitchen.*)

FRANK   (*to the audience*)There's no talking to her. Bloody Christmas. Christmas was invented for women. No, it was. You see it's like this, a woman likes to shop. A woman likes to send cards. A woman likes to play with fairy lights and decorate the house. A woman likes to complain that she's the only one that ever does anything at Christmas. And for some reason that completely escapes me – she loves every single bloody minute of it. But to a man, well Christmas is a living bloody hell.

                (JEAN *enters.*)

FRANK	Shopping at half past five in the morning – it's bloody ridiculous.
JEAN	I'm normally there on my own.
FRANK	And it was heaving.
JEAN	I wanted to go at four.
FRANK	Twelve pounds for a taxi.
JEAN	What do you want to do? Walk?
FRANK	Why do you leave everything until Christmas Eve?
JEAN	You can't buy your sprouts in August.
FRANK	Well that's a pity cos you've been shopping since bloody August. We hadn't touched down at Leeds / Bradford and we were in the duty free buying bloody Christmas presents.
JEAN	I was trying to save money.
FRANK	Then there was that Blue Cross sale in Debenhams,
JEAN	It was cheaper.
FRANK	It was April.
JEAN	They were bargains.
FRANK	(*to the audience*) She came in with about ten bags of bloody shopping. And she said, you'll never bloody believe this, "you'll never guess how much money I've saved us."
JEAN	I'd saved us a fortune.
FRANK	Call me old-fashioned Jean, but you'd just spent a bloody fortune.
JEAN	Right, well you do the shopping next year.

FRANK	I will.
JEAN	And then nobody'll get nowt.
FRANK	That's alright by me.
JEAN	Don't be stupid.
FRANK	I've told you what to do.
JEAN	You can't get a load of batteries, and wrap them up with a little note saying, 'toys not included'.
FRANK	Why not?
JEAN	Tight sod.
FRANK	You go bloody mad.
JEAN	It's what things cost.
FRANK	Spend far too much.
JEAN	You can't get stuff for nowt.
FRANK	It's a bloody racket, it really is. For one miserable day of the year.
JEAN	Miserable, I'll give you bloody miserable. Living with you, that's bloody miserable.
FRANK	Oh we're on to that now, are we?
JEAN	When is the last time you did anything nice for me?
FRANK	I was at Asda's at five-o'-bloody-clock this morning.
JEAN	That wasn't for me.
FRANK	Well who was it for then, the Man in the Moon?
JEAN	And I'm putting things in the basket and you're taking 'em back out.

FRANK	Nobody eats nuts.
JEAN	I do.
FRANK	Shit, Jean.
JEAN	You shit.

(Lights. Music – 'Rockin' Around The Christmas Tree'.)

Scene Two

Two hours later.

FRANK	How can I enjoy it, when Uncle Shithouse is coming again this year.
JEAN	He's my brother-in-law.
FRANK	I don't care if he was the bloody King of England, but five hours listening to the nautical pleasures of canal boating and I lost the will to live.
JEAN	Speed boating.
FRANK	I don't give a damn.
JEAN	And he's not that bad.
FRANK	Not that bad. I took the dog for a walk three times – and we haven't got a dog.
JEAN	You're awful, you.
FRANK	Awful, I got sick of hearing how much everything cost. Why doesn't he speak Engilsh.
JEAN	What're you talking about?
FRANK	Everthing's in bloody 'K'. Just bought that, Two-K. Bloody great boat, Fifty-K. Look at that, three-and-half-K if it was a penny.

JEAN   It's just the way he is.

FRANK   And then he only brings one bottle of wine.
            One bloody bottle of wine. One bottle of
            Blossom Hill, and then he drinks us out of
            house and home.

JEAN   He does not.

FRANK   And he's sex mad, he has his hands all over you.

JEAN   It's just you, you're a prune.

FRANK   Prude.

JEAN   You know what I mean.

FRANK   And Doreen'll be coming I expect.

JEAN   Well he's not coming on his own.

FRANK   She's got a face that can turn milk.

JEAN   She's my sister.

FRANK   I don't care who she is.

JEAN   You wanna lighten up.

FRANK   An' I'm hiding the Ferry Roshees. (*He means
            'Ferrero Rocher', but mispronounces.*)

JEAN   What?

FRANK   I don't mind the odd one, but last year she
            wouldn't stop.

JEAN   Have you heard yourself?

FRANK   Well I'm hiding 'em.

JEAN   It's a sweet, for God's sake.

FRANK   I'm hiding 'em.

JEAN   What happened to the season of Goodwill?

FRANK   Goodwill my arse. I have to play happy bloody
                 families with people I don't like.

JEAN   You don't like anybody.

FRANK   I don't like them.

JEAN   You're not that keen on yourself.

FRANK   You spend all your time calling her and then
                 you invite her for Christmas dinner.

JEAN   She's my sister.

FRANK   And they'll be bringing bloody Mastermind.

JEAN   Don't you talk about Alex like that.

FRANK   Oh come on, talk about thick, she couldn't
                 spell Bob backwards.

JEAN   Well we can't all be bloody clever.

ALEX   Coooo-eeee

JEAN   Speak of the devil.

FRANK   Good God.

                 (ALEX *enters through the kitchen.*)

ALEX   Hello, Auntie Jean. Uncle Frank.

FRANK   Hello, Alex. What a nice surprise!

ALEX   I can't come for dinner tomorrow.

JEAN   Oh no.

FRANK   Well that is devastating.

ALEX   Yeah.

JEAN   What a shame, we'll miss you, won't we, Frank.

FRANK   I'll not sleep tonight.

JEAN	Your mam and dad are still coming, though, aren't they?
ALEX	Yeah.
FRANK	Oh well, all is not lost, we've still got that little pleasure to look forward to.
JEAN	Have you had your Christmas present yet?
ALEX	Yeah.
	(*A beat.*)
JEAN	Nice?
ALEX	Yeah.
	(*A beat. It is a bit awkward.* JEAN *smiles, waiting for more of a response from* ALEX, *who merely smiles back.*)
FRANK	(*patronising*) What did you get?
ALEX	A car.
FRANK	A car!
JEAN	Fantastic. What sort of car?
ALEX	A red one.
FRANK	(*to the audience*) I know, it's bloody amazing. (*To* ALEX.) They're the best kind, red ones.
ALEX	I nearly bumped into this bus yesterday.
JEAN	Did ya?
ALEX	I tried slowing down, but I was still going too fast.
FRANK	What gear where you in?
ALEX	(*she thinks*) I was in my Nike shoes and my Gucci top.

(FRANK *looks to the audience, disgusted.*)

ALEX   Eeeh, I'm gonna have to get going.

FRANK   Oh what a shame.

JEAN   Are you sure you don't wanna a cup of tea or someat?

ALEX   (*gestures outside*) Me boyfriend's outside. We're going shopping.

FRANK   (*to audience*) I told you. Women, they love it.

JEAN   For your Christmas present.

ALEX   Yeah.

FRANK   What you getting, a Barbie doll?

ALEX   (*gesturing with her arm*) No.

FRANK   (*mimicking the same gesture*) Sorry.

ALEX   He's funny.

JEAN   Take no notice, pet, Christmas does this to him.

ALEX   Bye then.

            (*She kisses* JEAN.)

JEAN   Happy Christmas, Alex. You take care of yourself.

ALEX   Yeah. Happy Christmas, Uncle Frank.

            (*She kisses* FRANK.)

FRANK   It won't be the same without you tomorrow. We'll miss your stimulating conversation, won't we Jean?

ALEX   Bye then.

            (ALEX *exits through the kitchen.*)

FRANK   What the hell is all that about?

JEAN   Leave her.

FRANK   I could eat Alphabet soup and shit a better
                conversation than that.

JEAN   Stop being disgusting. She's harmless.

FRANK   Harmless. How do you work that out! She's
                bloody dangerous. She's gonna be let loose on
                the road with a car. They should make 'em do a
                test.

JEAN   She's passed her test.

FRANK   An intelligence test. If they can't speak in a
                sentence they don't pass.

JEAN   Don't talk so stupid.

FRANK   If they can't throw a constructive sentence
                together, bugger it, they don't drive.
                (*Mimicking her.*) Yeah. Yeah. Car. Red. Thank
                God for drugs that's all I can say.

                (*Lights and Music – 'Rockin' Around the
                Christmas Tree'.*)

Scene Three

Minutes later. JEAN *enters carrying the Radio Times.*

JEAN   You've left your *Radio Times* in the bag.

FRANK   *Christmas Radio Times* – This is a bloody
                waste of money.

JEAN   You've just bought it.

FRANK   It's a waste of money.

JEAN   What did you buy it for then?

FRANK   We buy it every year and it's a waste of
                money.

JEAN   You bought it.

FRANK   It's the same old rubbish every year.

JEAN   There's some good telly at Christmas.

FRANK   Who told you that?

JEAN   There's some good things on at Christmas.

FRANK   Listen, *The Great Escape*'ll be buried in here
            somewhere, If I see Steve McQueen on his
            motorbike one more Christmas I'm getting rid of
            that bloody telly.

JEAN   It's not that bad.

FRANK   Not that bad. Laurel and Hardy'll be on every
            sodding morning – followed by Charlie
            Chaplin. Who the hell finds Charlie Chaplin
            funny? It beats me, it really does. No it's a
            racket, it really is. (*Flicking through the
            magazine.*) Oh look at that.

JEAN   What?

FRANK   *It's a Wonderful Life.*

JEAN   Not with you it's not.

FRANK   On the telly. *It's a Wonderful Life* is on the
            telly again.

JEAN   Wasn't that on last year?

FRANK   It's on every bloody year, that's what I'm
            telling you. (*Looking in the magazine.*)
            Christmas Eve. *Santa Claus-the-bloody-Movie*,
            now there's some real imaginative scheduling.
            Oh good God I feel sick already.

            (FRANK *hears carol singers at the door.*)

FRANK   Carol singers.

JEAN   Where's me purse?

FRANK	You're not paying 'em.
JEAN	It's only carol singers.
FRANK	It's half past nine in the morning.
JEAN	They're only kids.
FRANK	Kids! Those little buggers have been coming round here since July.
JEAN	It's Christmas.
FRANK	They're not even singing. Have you heard that? They're not even singing a decent carol. 'Christmas is coming the pigs are getting fat', is not a carol. No bugger it. (*Exits. Voice, off.*) Go on, sod off. You're getting nowt here.

(FRANK *enters.*)

VOICE OF CAROL SINGER	(*off*) Bollocks, you tight sod.

(FRANK, *aghast, runs back out to the front door. He re-enters.*)

JEAN	You wanna calm down.
FRANK	I'm telling you, you pay one lot, they think you're a soft touch, they're back every bloody hour, and they tell all their mates, 'go to number 29, they give you someat'. Well I'm telling you there's no flies on me and they're getting bugger-all here.
JEAN	You wanna lighten up. You love Christmas, you always have done. I'll tell you what, we'll go to church this evening.
FRANK	Church!
JEAN	Get into the Christmas spirit.

FRANK	The only spirit I'll be getting into is a single malt – and plenty of 'em.
JEAN	It'll be nice in church with all the candles and the choir singing carols, oh, it'll be lovely.
FRANK	Look I'm worred about how much this bloody fiasco is going to cost us. You do know I'm not working, don't you.
JEAN	Is that's what this is all about?
FRANK	It's not a bottomless pit, Jean.
JEAN	We'll get by.
FRANK	The whole thing's spiralling out of bloody control.
JEAN	We'll get by, we always have.
FRANK	Get by. We've had to sell the car.
JEAN	Well that's your fault. I told you not to sell it. I said to you, "don't sell that car".
FRANK	And what the hell is it gonna run on, fresh air?
JEAN	You've got your redundancy money.
FRANK	We're saving that for a rainy day.
JEAN	Losing the bloody car is a rainy day, isn't it?
FRANK	Look, that's my redundancy money and you're not getting your hands on it, so there.
JEAN	Use a bit of your redundancy now, and then when you get a job, you can pay it back.
FRANK	But what if I can't get a bloody job?
JEAN	Of course you'll get a job.
FRANK	Don't be so bloody stupid. Who's gonna take me on at my age?

JEAN   Loads of people. You've just got to give it
        time. You can re-train, there's all sorts of
        things you can do.

FRANK   Re-train! What as? Come on, let's get into the
        real world, Jean, shall we? Re-train! Bloody
        brilliant. Hey, maybe I could get a job in
        Asda's. I'll start re-training now, shall I? (*He
        mimes a checkout moving items of food
        through the till.*) Beep. Beep. Beep. Hey, I'm a
        bloody natural. Maybe I don't need any bloody
        training. (*A sudden thought.*) And when it's
        Children in Need, I'll be able to get dressed
        up, and walk round the store dressed as a
        bloody Hobbit. (*Another sudden thought.*)

JEAN   You're being pathetic.

FRANK   Or what about the Post Office? (*He speaks in a
        sing song, automated sort of way.*) Cashier
        number three please. Cashier number two
        please. Cashier kiss my arse please.

JEAN   So that's what all the moaning's about?

FRANK   I'm being a realist, Jean.

JEAN   Look, a bit of redundancy doesn't have to spoil
        everything. Yes, it's a bloody nuisance and
        yes, you'd rather be at work, but bloody hell
        Frank, you're alright, aren't you? You've got
        your health haven't you?

FRANK   Well actually I've not been feeling too good –

JEAN   Good God, stop being so bloody pathetic.

FRANK   Are you a doctor then?

JEAN   You spoil every sodding thing.

FRANK   Are you a doctor then?

JEAN   Shit to you, Frank.

FRANK	You shit.
JEAN	I will.
FRANK	Good.

(*Lights and Music – 'Rockin' Around the Christmas Tree'.*)

Scene Four

One hour later. JEAN, *stood on a chair putting the finishes touches to the tree, turns and looks at him.* FRANK *has a string of fairy lights draped across the coffee table and is inspecting them*

FRANK	Bloody fairy lights. (*Pause.*) Bloody, bloody fairy lights. Bloody sodding fairy lights. (*A beat.*) I don't know why you don't put things away properly.
JEAN	Why I put things away!
FRANK	Yes. Then we wouldn't have this bloody carry on every year. Planning ahead, Jean, that's what you need to do.
JEAN	Do I, now?
FRANK	If you'd put these away carefully –
JEAN	Who are you talking to?
FRANK	I'm just saying, you need to learn to plan a bit better.
JEAN	I'll plan your bloody arse for you in a minute.
FRANK	I'm just saying.
JEAN	Well don't.
FRANK	Nothing works in this bloody house. You bought that Advent Calendar from Grimsby and all the windows were boarded up. Ah, there it

is, the little bugger. I need a new bulb. Get me
a new bulb.

(JEAN *turns and looks at him.*)

JEAN   What!

FRANK   (*impatiently*) Come on. (*He snaps his fingers
              impatiently.*)

              (*She gets down off the chair and walks over to
              the box of Christmas decorations, and takes
              out a bulb.*)

              (*talking to the dud bulb*) It's you, you little
              bugger.

JEAN   There we go.

              (JEAN *resumes her position on the chair and
              puts some more decorations on the tree.* FRANK
              notices another bulb.)

FRANK   Oh bloody hell, I need another one. Can you
              get me another one?

              (*A beat.* JEAN *looks at him. He snaps his
              fingers once more.*)

              I need another one.

JEAN   Can't you get one out of the box?

FRANK   Then I'll forget where I'm up to.

              (JEAN *gets down off the chair and gets him
              another one out of the box.*)

JEAN   Right, I'll stop what I'm doing and I'll get down
              off the chair and I'll get you one.

FRANK   There's no need to be like that.

JEAN   I might as well do it myself. I ask you to do one
              thing this year and you've done nowt but
              complain since you started.

FRANK   Am I complainin'?

JEAN   You've done nowt but complain.

FRANK   I don't know why we have to bother with
             decorations.

JEAN   It's Christmas.

FRANK   Who wants to look at a plastic tree draped with
             tinsel? Come on, Jean, we've grown out of it.

FRANK   There, they're bloody finished.

JEAN   Hadn't you better test them?

FRANK   I don't need to test 'em.

JEAN   They won't work.

FRANK   Course they'll work.

JEAN   Well test 'em then.

FRANK   I'm not testing 'em.

JEAN   Right, well get the rest of the decorations out
             of the box.

FRANK   Do we have to bother with all this lot?

JEAN   Yes.

FRANK   Bloody decorations.

             (FRANK *pulls out a snowman.*)

             We're not putting this bloody thing out again
             are we?

JEAN   (*delighted*) Frosty. It's Frosty. We have to
             have Frosty out.

FRANK   It works when it isn't supposed to, then
             doesn't when it should. It drives you bloody
             bananas.

JEAN	Put him down.
FRANK	No!
JEAN	Put him down.
FRANK	(*reluctantly plugging him in*) Bloody stupid thing.
JEAN	Careful with him, he's ten years old this Christmas. Fifty-eight in Frosty years.
FRANK	Oh for God's sake.
JEAN	Now bang something. Go on. Clap your hands.
FRANK	(*to the audience*) Why me?
JEAN	Go on.
	(FRANK *reluctantly claps his hands. Nothing.*)
JEAN	It's 'cos he knows you don't love him.
FRANK	Oh for God's sake.
	(JEAN *claps her hands. The Snowman illuminates and wobbles his body singing Frosty the Snowman. She sings along with him, laughing and enjoying him. The more she enjoys it the more irritated* FRANK *becomes.*)
JEAN	Isn't he good?
FRANK	(*sarcastically*) Brilliant.
	(FRANK *claps his hands to stop him. Nothing. He claps his hands a few more times getting quite manic. He gives up.* JEAN *claps her hands – he stops.*)
FRANK	If he plays up this year he's going through the window, I'm telling you.
	(FRANK *pulls a Santa out of the box.*)

Oh, I don't believe this.

JEAN   (*excited*) Santa! Put him down and clap your
                hands.

FRANK   No.

JEAN   Go on.

FRANK   I'm not.

JEAN   Oh go on.

FRANK   Bugger off.

                (FRANK *puts him down and walks away.*)

JEAN   Right! I'll do it then, misery. It's being so
                happy that keeps you going.

                (JEAN *puts him down on the sideboeard and
                claps her hands. Santa plays 'Jingle Bells'
                and the Snowman sings 'Frosty the Snowman'.*
                JEAN *laughs uproariously.*)

FRANK   (*to the audience*) Well that's cheered me up no
                end. Isn't that absolutely bloody terrific. Oh
                yes, it's gonna be a fun-packed bloody
                Christmas this year.

                (FRANK *claps his hands nothing happens.* JEAN
                claps, they stop. FRANK, *annoyed, sits on the
                settee.*)

JEAN   What else is in there?

FRANK   Well it's bound to be bloody exciting whatever
                it is.

                (JEAN *is shocked with what she pulls out of the
                box. She is overcome.*)

JEAN   Oh no.

FRANK   What?

JEAN	Oh . . .
FRANK	(*growing impatient*) What?
JEAN	It's . . . it's her three-legged cow. And the rest of the nativity. The one she made in nursery. (JEAN *looks back into the box.*) Oh, I don't believe it.
FRANK	What?
JEAN	Her Angel.

(JEAN *pulls a quite sizeable Angel out of the box. It looks obviously made by a small child. It has great sentimental value to* JEAN.)

I've been looking everywhere for her Angel.

FRANK	Well if you'd planned ahead.
JEAN	Oh God!
FRANK	Oh bloody hell, don't start.
JEAN	Put it up Frank.
FRANK	Where?

(*A beat. Through tears* JEAN *turns and looks at* FRANK.)

JEAN	On the tree. Where the hell do you think? Where!
FRANK	I don't know, it could be any-bloody-where with you.

(FRANK *climbs on to the chair and puts the Angel on top of the tree.*)

JEAN	She was only small when she made that Angel. She made her with her tiny little hands and her tiny little fingers.
FRANK	There. (FRANK *climbs down and admires his work.*) Do you think it's leaning a bit?

JEAN   She should be here, Frank. She should be here
                with us. (*A beat.*) It's Christmas eve and she
                should be here. Santa would put new pyjamas
                on her pillow on Christmas eve and she used to
                get so excited, she'd be ready for bed in the
                middle of the afternoon.

FRANK   Lets go and find her, Jean.

JEAN   We can't.

FRANK   Course we can.

JEAN   She said she didn't want to see us again.

FRANK   She didn't mean it.

JEAN   Well why hasn't she been in touch then?
                We've never heard a word from her.

FRANK   We'll find her and talk to her . . .

JEAN   We can't. Let's face it, Frank. She's disowned
                us. She said she wanted nowt to do with us
                ever again. Can't you get that through your
                thick head?

FRANK   You're just being bloody stubborn, that's your
                trouble.

                (*A beat.*)

JEAN   You think it's my fault, don't you?

FRANK   I just want . . .

JEAN   You do.

FRANK   I don't.

JEAN   You blame me.

FRANK   I don't

JEAN   I can see you looking at me.

FRANK   Good God, I've got to look at you, I bloody live
            with you.

JEAN   But you do look at me, you stare at me and I
            know you blame me.

FRANK   I've never said that.

JEAN   You don't have to, it's written all over your
            bloody face.

FRANK   What have I done?

JEAN   If you don't like it, why don't you leave.

FRANK   I haven't said a bloody word.

JEAN   If I'm that bloody stubborn. If I'm that bloody
            unreasonable why don't you get out?

FRANK   What the hell are you talking about?

JEAN   You don't like me. I get no support from you.
            And you blame me. I know you do. An' I try to
            ignore it and I try to keep upbeat. I'm trying to
            keep everything normal and all you do is
            complain and I can't cope with it anymore. An'
            I don't know how I'm gonna get through
            Christmas. Nothing I do is right for you, is it?
            Nothing. Well I'm fed up with it. You can stick
            your Christmas up your arse, do you hear me?
            Pig!

            (*Frosty snaps into life, singing 'Frosty the
            Snowman'.*)

FRANK   Hey, come on.

JEAN   Don't you dare come near me.

FRANK   Look, we'll get by, we always have. Look, I'll
            put the lights on the tree. (FRANK *picks up the
            fairy lights and starts to wrap them round the
            tree.*) Look, we'll have a good time. And I'll
            cook the turkey this year. Did you hear? You

won't have to do a thing. Hey, these are
looking good, aren't they? Yes, you leave it to
me. You have a rest, enjoy yourself – well, you
know, we'll have a good time even if it kills me.
There. Any bald patches? Have I missed any?
Ang' on, there's a bit. (*He makes a slight
alteration.*) There, that's better. What do you
think? Right, I'll switch 'em on. (*He moves to
the light switch.*) I now declare these tree
lights officially open.

(*He switches them on. The lights pop and
Santa Claus starts singing 'Jingle Bells' and
Frosty stops singing.* JEAN, *crying runs out.*)

FRANK   Bloody hell! (FRANK *exits after her.*) Jean, come
             here.

             (*Lights and Music. Shakin' Stevens – 'Rock
             'n' Roll Christmas'.*)

Scene Five

Christmas morning, 9.00 AM. FRANK *enters into the kitchen
wearing a Santa hat and a ridiculous pinny with the body of a
bikini-clad woman on it. He is singing, carrying a turkey in a
baking tray and a can of beer. He thinks for a moment, checks
to see if anyone is there and cheekily pours a bit of his beer
over the turkey. He puts the turkey down on the kitchen bench
and dances into the living room. He eats a nut. He is
thoroughly enjoying himself. He becomes Shakin' Stevens,
singing and dancing to the music. Pleased with himself,* FRANK
starts to take a drink when JEAN *enters carrying a big dish of
Ferrero Rocher . . .*

JEAN   What the hell are you doing?

             (FRANK, *startled, jumps.*)

FRANK   I'm having a drink.

JEAN   It's nine o'clock in the morning.

FRANK   It's Christmas Day.

JEAN	Our Doreen's coming.
FRANK	It's only a beer.
JEAN	Have you put the turkey in?
FRANK	I'm doing it now.
JEAN	I've given you one job to do.
FRANK	I'm putting it in now.
JEAN	I've done every bloody thing else.
FRANK	I'm doing it.
JEAN	And you can't do that.
FRANK	I am.
JEAN	It's not too much to ask, is it. One little thing. And what the hell is it doing in the front room. You're supposed to be helping me. You know if you want anything doing in this house you have to do it yourself.
FRANK	(*marching down stage to the audience*) She's gonna bloody get it in a minute.
JEAN	Have you basted it?
FRANK	I thought I was doing the bird this year?
JEAN	Is it basted?
FRANK	Just leave it to me as agreed.
JEAN	You haven't basted it.
FRANK	(*raising his voice*) I have bloody basted it.
JEAN	There's no need to raise your voice, it's Christmas Day.
FRANK	(*a little louder*) I know, it's Christmas Day, that's why I'm putting the turkey in.

JEAN   Have you stuffed it?

FRANK   I'll bloody stuff you in a minute.

JEAN   You haven't stuffed it, have you?

FRANK   Do the bugger yourself.

JEAN   There's no need to be bloody nasty.

FRANK   No, I'm fed up with you.

JEAN   I'm only trying to help.

FRANK   Have you done this, have you done that . . .

JEAN   It should have been in by now.

FRANK   And it would have been if you hadn't started
            bloody interfering.

JEAN   Don't you speak to me like that.

            (JEAN *exits into the kitchen to tend to the
            turkey.*)

FRANK   It's bloody Christmas Day again, isn't it?

FRANK   (*calling off*) I said I was going to do the turkey,
            but you can't do it, can you? You can't let me
            do anything. You have to bloody interfere.

JEAN   (*off*) I can hear you.

FRANK   Good. (*To audience.*) You know what her
            problem is, she's not happy unless she's
            stressed. Well she can shit as far as I'm
            concerned.

            (FRANK *produces another can of lager from his
            trouser pocket.* JEAN *enters and they exchange
            a look.* FRANK *lifts the can up in front of her
            and provocatively opens it. He then moves
            away and sits down. And in a childish display
            of temper makes a point of turning his back*

on her. He is in a mood. JEAN *sighs. She tries to make amends.*)

JEAN   I've put the turkey in. (*A beat.*) Doreen's coming and I just wanted to have things right, you know what I mean.

(JEAN *goes and gets him a present.*)

JEAN   Here.

(*A beat. He looks at the present and then up at her.*)

FRANK   What's this?

JEAN   It's your present.

(*A beat. A look of fear creeps across* FRANK'S *face.*)

FRANK   (*nervously*) I th . . . I th . . . ought we weren't getting each other presents this year.

JEAN   It's only a little one.

FRANK   We agreed.

JEAN   It's just someat small.

FRANK   The carpet was our present to the both of us.

JEAN   You have to have someat to open on Christmas Day.

FRANK   You haven't.

(*A beat.*)

JEAN   Haven't you got me owt?

FRANK   We said we won't buy presents this year, 'cos we haven't got much money, what with me not working an' that.

JEAN   Nothing at all.

FRANK	The carpet, the bloody carpet, that's your present. Do you want me to put a ribbon on it?
JEAN	I can't believe you haven't got me a little surprise.
FRANK	You didn't say you wanted one.
JEAN	If I said I wanted one it wouldn't be a surprise, would it.
FRANK	I'll get you someat tomorrow.
JEAN	Forget it.
FRANK	It'll be half price tomorrow.
JEAN	It doesn't matter.
FRANK	I'll get you twice as much.
JEAN	You never do anything nice for me.
FRANK	I got you the carpet.
JEAN	That's not for me.
FRANK	Who's it for then, Father-bloody-Christmas?
JEAN	Shit, Frank.
FRANK	You shit.
	(*A beat.*)
FRANK	Well if you take this back we'll both be the same.
	(*Pause.*)
	Shall I open it?
JEAN	Pig.
FRANK	Look, I'll get you something tomorrow.
JEAN	Don't talk to me.

(JEAN *walks away.*)

FRANK   (*to audience*) I could spit, I really could. (*To*
             JEAN.) Alright, I'll open it. I'm opening it.

             (JEAN *sulks.* FRANK *opens the present. It is a*
             hideous jumper with a picture of a large
             reindeer face, complete with antlers and
             illuminating nose. He gives a disgusted look
             to the audience before feigning pleasure.)

FRANK   Oh this is gorgeous.

             (*A beat.* JEAN *begins to melt.*)

             Oh I like this.

JEAN   What?

FRANK   This is gorgeous.

JEAN   Yeah, well.

FRANK   What a great present.

JEAN   Do you like it?

FRANK   When people see me in this, they'll all want one.

JEAN   Does it fit?

FRANK   I thought I might save it for a special occasion.

JEAN   It's Christmas morning, you daft bugger, now
             gerrit on.

             (FRANK *takes off his pinny and puts it on.*)

             Sheila said it wasn't you but I think it goes
             with your sunny disposition.

             (*It is huge. He wafts his arms around and the*
             long ends of the sleeve flap well over the ends
             of his hands.)

FRANK   Like a glove.

(JEAN *sorts it out*.)

JEAN	It just needs a bit of sorting out. There, do you like it?
FRANK	It's gorgeous.
JEAN	You'll be able to wear it when you go down to the pub.

(FRANK *looks to the audience*.)

FRANK	I'll look forward to that, then.
JEAN	I had it specially made.
FRANK	(*to himself*) Who by, the blind school?
JEAN	What?
FRANK	Makes me feel really cool.
JEAN	I knew you'd like it.
FRANK	And I'll get you something tomorrow.
JEAN	It does suit you, that jumper.
FRANK	I know. I mean that carpet cost eight hundred pounds.
JEAN	It did not.
FRANK	Didn't it?
JEAN	No.
FRANK	Well I don't know how much it bloody cost. When we left the shop I could have sworn it was eight hundred pounds.
JEAN	What about the underlay.
FRANK	The underlay was included.
JEAN	Are you arguing with me?
FRANK	No.

JEAN	Good. I'm not having you embarrass me in front of our Doreen.
FRANK	Bloody hell.
JEAN	I'm not having you spoil today.
FRANK	I'm not.
JEAN	You'd better not.
FRANK	I'm not.
JEAN	'Cos I'm warning you. And for God's sake don't mention that we had to sell the car.
FRANK	I won't.
JEAN	You'd better not.
FRANK	Alright.
JEAN	Got it?
FRANK	Yes
JEAN	Right then.
FRANK	Right then.
JEAN	Lets start again, shall we? (*Quite aggressive.*) Happy Christmas.
FRANK	(*quite aggressive*) Happy Christmas. (*To the audience.*) I could bloody swing for her, I could. (*Music: Shakin' Stevens – 'Rock 'n' Roll Christmas'.*)

Scene Six

10.30 AM. JEAN *enters the living room.*

JEAN   Right, that's the table's all set for dinner. It
                looks lovely. It's like a work of art. I think
                those little gold hearts set it off. (*There is no
                reaction from* FRANK. *A beat.* JEAN *tries
                another approach.*) Hey!

FRANK   (*very aggressively*) What?

                (JEAN, *shocked by the severity of his reply, tuts.*)

JEAN   Tut. (*Cheekily.*) Shall we open the Buck's Fizz?

FRANK   I thought it was a bit early for drink.

JEAN   Sod it, it's Christmas.

FRANK   That's what I said.

JEAN   Well do you want one or not?

FRANK   Yes, course I do.

                (JEAN *scampers out to get the drinks.*)

FRANK   (*to audience*) We always have the Buck's Fizz!
                Every Christmas morning we have the Buck's
                Fizz. An' you know why – 'cos we don't care.
                It's a kind of tradition in our house. Well if you
                can't enjoy yourself on Christmas morning,
                when can you?

                (JEAN *enters, carrying two glasses of Buck's
                Fizz.*)

JEAN   There ya go.

FRANK   Cheers.

JEAN   Cheers.

JEAN   Ooh, that's lovely. Nice 'n cold. I've had it on
                ice – (*Proudly.*) in the ice bucket.

FRANK   (*to the audience*) I didn't know we had a
                bloody ice bucket. (*To* JEAN.) Good stuff, that,
                Jean.

JEAN	I hope you're not gonna be crying this year, watching Noel Edmonds.
	(FRANK, *shocked, looks to the audience to check if they've heard.*)
FRANK	I've never cried.
JEAN	You cry every year watching Noel Edmonds' *Christmas Surprises*.
FRANK	(*to audience*) I don't.
JEAN	Blubber like a big bloody baby.
FRANK	Jean, I do not cry watching Noel Edmonds. Anyway, he finished years ago.
JEAN	Do you wanna mince pie?
FRANK	I haven't had me breakfast.
JEAN	So?
FRANK	Bloody mince pie for breakfast.
JEAN	(*teasing him*) Marks and Spencers . . .
	(FRANK *is shocked.*)
FRANK	Marks and Spencers!
JEAN	Yeah.
FRANK	For me.
JEAN	Yeah.
FRANK	Oh go on then. (*To audience, excited.*) I bloody love Christmas. I'm not usually allowed to have 'em. You see, she buys two lots, some from Asda, they're for us, and some from Marks and Spencers – but they are only for the guests.

(JEAN *returns with the mince pies.*)

JEAN   Only the one, mind.

FRANK   (*eating the pie*) Mmmm, this is gorgeous. I
            bloody love Marks and Spencer's.

JEAN   You ate a whole box one Christmas morning –
            can you remember? And you were sick all over
            your new slippers.

FRANK   I was.

JEAN   I can't smell the turkey.

FRANK   Give it chance, it's just gone in.

JEAN   It's probably 'cos it's so big.

FRANK   (*to audience*) Biggest in the shop.

JEAN   I couldn't get it in the fridge.

FRANK   It was that big last year, we were still eating it
            at Easter.

            (*They laugh.*)

JEAN   Hey, come on.

FRANK   What?

JEAN   I'll have to get hoovering.

FRANK   It's Christmas Day.

JEAN   I'm not having people coming round and the
            place being a mess.

FRANK   It looks alright.

JEAN   The hoover, Frank.

FRANK   I'm not.

JEAN   I'm warning you.

FRANK   Anyway, that hoover's knackered.

JEAN	I told you we needed a new one. You said we couldn't afford one.
FRANK	We can't.
JEAN	(*noticing him*) An' I hope you're getting changed.
FRANK	What?
JEAN	You're not wearing those trousers.
FRANK	What's the matter with 'em?
JEAN	I'm not having you showing me up.
FRANK	What?
JEAN	You can put your new suit on.
FRANK	Sod off.
JEAN	It was made to measure.
FRANK	Yeah, but I think it was made to measure some bugger else.
JEAN	Have you got your new underpants on?
FRANK	Yes. And they're right up me bloody arse.
JEAN	I told you to get a bigger size.
FRANK	(*forceful*) I'm a medium.
JEAN	Well, I've made an effort.
FRANK	Good.
JEAN	You're not bloody interested, are you?
FRANK	I am.
JEAN	Well, do you like it?

FRANK	What?
JEAN	Me outfit, it's new, do you like it?
FRANK	(*uninterested*) Brilliant.
JEAN	You don't think this dress makes me look fat, do you?
FRANK	No, that's got nowt to do with your dress, it's your big fat arse . . . (*She snaps a glare at him.*) No, of course it doesn't.
JEAN	What did you say?
FRANK	I'll just check on the turkey.
CAROL SINGERS	(*off*) 'We Wish You a Merry Christmas, We Wish You a Merry Christmas and a Happy New Year' . . . (*Etc.*)
FRANK	They're here.
JEAN	Who?
FRANK	Doreen and Harry. (*Aside to audience.*) They do this every bloody year, pretend to be carol singers.
JEAN	Bloody hell they're early. How do I look?
FRANK	Fine.
JEAN	Have you done the sprouts?
FRANK	I haven't had time.
JEAN	I give you one job to do.
FRANK	I'll do 'em later.
JEAN	When?
FRANK	I don't bloody know.
JEAN	You better get 'em done.

FRANK   Stick a brush up me arse and I'll sweep the
               path while I'm at it.

JEAN   I should've done 'em meself.

FRANK   I'm letting 'em in.

JEAN   I wanted to hoover.

FRANK   I'm letting 'em in.

               (FRANK *exits.* JEAN *fusses around and them,
               takes a deep breath and switches into relaxed
               mode.*)

FRANK   (*off*) Not today, thank you. Doreen! Harry! I
               thought you were carol singers. By you had me
               fooled then.

HARRY   (*off*) 'We wish you a Merry Christmas, We wish
               you a Merry Christmas, We wish . . . '

DOREEN   (*off*) Harry! Calm down. Happy Christmas,
               Frank.

FRANK   (*off*) I've been dying for you to get here. Come
               on in.

               (FRANK *re-enters.*)

               It isn't carol singers, it's Harry and Doreen.

               (DOREEN *and* HARRY, *followed by* FRANK, *enter
               the room. They exchange Christmas greetings.*)

HARRY   (*to* JEAN) Come here, you little sex kitten.
               (*They embrace.*) You look younger every year.
               Hey, she looks younger every year. It's a good
               job I'm married.

               (HARRY *gooses her when she breaks free. She
               emits a little whoop.*)

JEAN   Harry!

HARRY   What goes like a tiger and winks?

JEAN   I dunno.

            (HARRY *winks*.)

JEAN   Eee you're terrible. What are you after?

DOREEN   He's after a good hiding and he'll get one if he
            carries on like that. We're not too early, are we,
            Jean?

JEAN   No, of course not, we've been sat round,
            kicking our heels waiting for you to arrive.

HARRY   Oh my God, Frank, what the hell have you got
            on? Have you seen this, Doreen? That is a
            bugger.

FRANK   Jean got me it.

            (JEAN *and* DOREEN *stare at* HARRY.)

HARRY   That is a bugger of a nice jumper, that.

DOREEN   Harry, swearing. You know I can't abide
            swearing. If there's one thing I can't abide,
            it's swearing.

JEAN   Christmas wouldn't be the same without you
            here, Doreen. I was just saying to Frank wasn't
            I, Frank?

FRANK   I've been looking forward to it for weeks.

DOREEN   Well it has become something of a Christmas
            tradition.

FRANK   (*smiling through gritted teeth*) It certainly
            bloody has.

DOREEN   Ee, this place doesn't change does it? You
            always have it nice. It's worn well this three
            piece suite, hasn't it. How many years have
            you had this now?

(HARRY *is hovering near the window looking at his car.* JEAN *glowers at the back of her head.* FRANK *mimes throttling* DOREEN.)

Ooh, Ferrero Rocher, my favourite. (*She picks one off the dish, unwraps it and then eats it.*) You know I really shouldn't. Plays havoc with the Atkins. I really shouldn't.

FRANK   Go on, force yourself.

HARRY   Is my car safe there? You know you can't be too careful round here.

JEAN   What?

HARRY   No offence, but you know that little machine out there does nought to sixty in seven seconds. Thirty-K if it was a penny.

FRANK   Thirty-K!

HARRY   Maybe I should go and park it on the Avenue. I think it would be safer on the Avenue.

FRANK   Why don't you put it in the garage?

JEAN   (*shocked*) Frank, it's because our car's in the garage.

FRANK   (*laughing, to* HARRY) Silly me. (*To the audience.*) Bloody hell.

DOREEN   These are lovely.

(DOREEN *goes for another Ferrero Rocher.*)

DOREEN   I shouldn't you know. I really shouldn't.

FRANK   No, but you bloody are.

JEAN   Frank!

HARRY   Oh, I've brought you some drink.

FRANK   (*surprised*) Have you?

JEAN   Oh you shouldn't have bothered.

HARRY   That's what Doreen said, she said they'll be
             insulted if we start taking drink over.

FRANK   No, we wouldn't.

HARRY   That's what I said. It's Christmas. And it is
             better to give than to receive. So there you go.

             (FRANK *and* JEAN *exchange a glance.* HARRY
             produces one bottle of wine in a wine bag.
             FRANK *pulls the bottle out of the bag.*)

FRANK   Blossom Hill. Well that is a nice surprise. Look
             Jean, they've brought us one bottle of Blossom
             Hill. (*Reading the label on the bottle.*) A soft
             and fruity Californian red. Brilliant. Well the
             four of us will certainly party into the night
             with this, won't we.

             (HARRY'S *phone rings. His ring tone is 'Sex
             Bomb' by Tom Jones.*)

HARRY   Excuse me. Yeah, yeah. I don't care if it's
             Christmas Day, this is costing me money, get
             them out. No, I haven't got time to discuss it
             now.

JEAN   Fancy that, on Christmas Day 'n all.

HARRY   Sorry about that, the wheels of industry, Jean.

FRANK   Can I get anybody a drink?

HARRY   I thought you'd never ask. Bring it on.

FRANK   (*to the audience*) He can't bloody wait.

JEAN   We're having the Buck's Fizz, Doreen.

DOREEN   I don't mean to be cheeky, but is it decent
             champagne, 'cos that cheap stuff plays havoc
             with my indigestion.

HARRY   Oh, and once she starts blowing off, bloody
               hell.

DOREEN   Is there any need?

HARRY   She's like a brass band.

DOREEN   Harry!

HARRY   And the bloody smell.

DOREEN   I'm warning you.

FRANK   Well there's no worries there Doreen pet, no
               cheap rubbish in this house. Good stuff this,
               Asti Spew-manti.

DOREEN   What!

HARRY   I'll give you a hand, Frank.

               (*As they exit,* FRANK *picks up the Ferrero
               Rocher and takes them out with him.*)

JEAN   Frank!

               (FRANK, *in the one sweeping movement, turns
               and puts them back. They then exit up centre
               to the dining room.*)

JEAN   Eee, I'm forgetting me manners, let me take
               your coat, Doreen.

               (*She helps* DOREEN *take off her coat.*)

DOREEN   Jean, could you put it on a hanger, it's just I
               don't want it to lose its shape.

JEAN   (*calling to* FRANK) Nip up and get me a coat
               hanger for Doreen's coat, will you, Frank?

FRANK   (*off*) Just hang it in the hall.

JEAN   A coat hanger, Frank.

DOREEN   Oh I see you've got the same artificial tree as
             last year, Jean.

JEAN   Well, it doesn't drop, Doreen.

DOREEN   It's not the same though, is it, Jean.

JEAN   What?

DOREEN   As a real tree. I mean you can't beat a real tree.

JEAN   I can't stand the needles, they get everywhere.

DOREEN   Oh, Scotch Pines don't drop, Jean and they're
             not old-fashioned.

JEAN   Old-fashioned!

DOREEN   Well, I mean, with all due respect, Jean, it's not
             co-ordinated, is it. Ours is red and gold, to
             match the red candles in the gold holders we
             have on the mantel piece. Design is everything
             these days, Jean. You don't just throw a tree
             together . . .

JEAN   Thrown together . . .

DOREEN   . . . it's a work of art and it doesn't do to be too
             busy.

JEAN   Bloody busy!

DOREEN   Oh you must think I'm terribly rude, we haven't
             given you your present. (*Calling off.*) Harry,
             their present.

JEAN   Oh Doreen, we don't expect a present.

             (HARRY *and* FRANK *re-enter with drinks and a
             coat hanger.*)

DOREEN   Nonsense, Jean, It's just a little something. It's
             nice to have a little something to open on
             Christmas morning, isn't it?

JEAN   (*pointedly at* FRANK) Yes it is.

FRANK	(*he hands the drinks round*) There you go.
HARRY	Here it is. It's for the both of you.
	(*He hands over the present to* FRANK. *He opens the present.*)
FRANK	Well this is exciting, isn't it. (*He reveals the present.*) A car alarm. Well that's great, isn't it! Look Jean, a car alarm. For protecting the car.
DOREEN	Well you can't be too careful round here, can you.
JEAN	It's not Beirut, you know.
FRANK	It's lovely Doreen. That'll come in really useful, won't it, Jean? We'll put that in the car.
HARRY	(*hovering near the window*) It's gonna snow, I knew we should have come in a taxi.
JEAN	Well here's to it.
	(*They all toast Happy Christmas.*)
	(*Music: Shakin' Stevens – 'Rock 'n' Roll Christmas'.*)

Scene Seven

One hour later.

FRANK	Have you ever had one of those moments when you just think things can't get any worse.
VOICE	(*off*) Happy Christmas!
FRANK	And then they do. Our next door neighbours arrived. They've only been in a couple of months and already it feels like years.

                (GARY *enters, a big bruiser of a bloke. He*
                carries an unusually large bottle of beer
                which he drinks from. He throws his arms in
                the air star-like and bellows.)

GARY   Lets get ready to rumble. (*He farts.*) Ooh that's
                loosened it.

                (DOREEN *and* JEAN *are suitably disgusted.*
                HARRY *enjoys it.*)

HARRY   Nice one.

                (DOREEN *snaps to* HARRY, *who instantly loses*
                his grin.)

GARY   Eee, I'm sorry, I've got an arse like a Japanese
                sunset. Happy Christmas, Frank.

                (FRANK *goes to shake his hand,* GARY *bobs and*
                throws a lightning punch that has the desired
                effect – it doesn't connect, but nonetheless
                unnerves FRANK. FRANK *laughs nervously.*)

GARY   Hey!

                (*He turns to* JEAN.)

                Happy Christmas, Jean.

                (*He kisses her, and turns to* DOREEN.)

                Oh yes . . . (*Indicating the resemblance to*
                JEAN.) . . . you look so much alike.

DOREEN   I can't see it myself.

GARY   Oh yes, I can. (*Implying* DOREEN.) This must be
                your mother, is it?

JEAN   Sister.

GARY   Is it?

DOREEN   Younger sister, actually.

HARRY   She had a hard paper round.

               (DOREEN *snaps her head and glares at him.*
               HARRY *quickly wipes the smile off his face.*)

               You look beautiful, darling.

GARY   Happy Christmas anyway.

DOREEN   Mother!

JEAN   (*to* GARY) Where's Julie?

GARY   She's coming, don't you worry about that.

FRANK   (*sarcastically*) Oh Good.

               (GARY *turns to* HARRY. HARRY *introduces
               himself.*)

HARRY   Harry. All the best.

               (*He shakes* HARRY'S *hand and squashes it.*)

GARY   And you.

               (HARRY *clenches his bruised hand and at the
               same time tries to laugh it off.*)

DOREEN   Bloody mother!

FRANK   (*to* GARY, *who has a bandage round his hand*)
               What happened to your hand?

GARY   Last night in the pub. By hell, we sunk some.
               I'll tell you what! And then this piece of scum,
               came on to my wife. Now that annoys me. I
               hate people taking advantage. You see, I know
               I don't look it, but I'm the jealous type.
               Anybody touches our lass and I can't help it, a
               mist comes over my eyes and I lose it. This
               turd decided to put his hands all over our lass
               and and so I decided to put my fist all over his
               face.

FRANK   Might as well get into the Season of Goodwill
               early.

GARY   I mean, Julie wouldn't hurt a fly. She's a little
               Angel.

HARRY   You're lucky Doreen's still alive.

               (*They all laugh.* DOREEN *a little later joins in
               and forces out a laugh also and speaks
               through gritted teeth.*)

DOREEN   Just wait 'til I get you home.

HARRY   It was a joke.

GARY   It's just that you have to be careful with her
               being in her condition.

FRANK   What condition?

GARY   Nobody's supposed to know but (*Confiding in
               them.*) – she's nearly pregnant.

               (*A beat. They are all confused.*)

FRANK   Come again.

GARY   Well we're trying for a family. We've been at it
               all night.

HARRY   (*impressed*) Have you?

GARY   I can barely walk this morning.

HARRY   How do you manage to go all . . .

DOREEN   Harry!

HARRY   (*snapping out of it*) Disgusting.

               (*He slugs his beer.* JULIE *enters shrieking and
               laughing. She is very brassy. Her chest leaves
               little to the imagination, and her heels are*

high and her skirt is short. All her clothes are
a little too tight. She blows a party squeaker.)

JULIE   Happy Christmas, everybody.

HARRY   Bloody hell!

DOREEN   Good grief, it's Madam Sin.

JULIE   Frankie boy, this could be your lucky day.

FRANK   (*to the audience*) I have this strange feeling
             she couldn't be further from the truth. (*To*
             JULIE.) You don't say.

             (JULIE *reveals some mistletoe from behind her*
             back and dangles it teasingly above her
             head.)

FRANK   (*looks at* GARY *and then at* JULIE – *he gulps*)
             Oh God.

JEAN   Well go on then, Frank.

             (FRANK *glares at* JEAN. *He stutters and*
             stammers his way through. HARRY *enjoys it.*)

FRANK   Well . . . you know . . . there . . . you go . . .

HARRY   Go on, Frank, give her one from m . . . (GARY
             and DOREEN *look to* HARRY, *who goes to the*
             window to check on his car.) It does look like
             snow.

FRANK   . . . I'm a bit shy . . . deary me . . . all the best.

             (*He offers to shake her hand. She grabs him*
             and kisses him. He parts, somewhat
             dishevelled.)

FRANK   Well that was very nice.

GARY   You what!

FRANK   No it wasn't, it was horrible.

JULIE   You what!

FRANK   Not horrible, it was . . . well it was okay.

                 (JULIE *and* GARY *point to him laughing. They
                 were having a joke.* FRANK *is somewhat
                 relieved.*)

FRANK   Would you like a drink, Julie? We're having the
                 Buck's Fizz.

JULIE   Go on then, as long as it's a large one.

                 (*She laughs.*)

GARY   Aye, go on, while you're at it.

FRANK   Would you like the Buck's Fizz?

GARY   Are you taking the piss out of me?

FRANK   No, I just thought . . .

                 (GARY *points at* FRANK *and laughs.* HARRY,
                 relieved, pathetically joins in.)

FRANK   Right. (*To the audience.*) Bloody hell!

                 (FRANK *exits to get some drinks.*)

JULIE   Oh, and who is this handsome looking young
                 man?

                 (HARRY *is flattered.*)

HARRY   It's me.

JULIE   Well come on then, big boy.

DOREEN   (*referring to the size of his manhood*) Ooh, I
                 don't think so.

JULIE   Come on.

                 (JULIE *waggles her chest.*)

DOREEN   That's one thing he's not.

GARY   (*to* HARRY) She is a knock out, isn't she.

HARRY   Hilarious.

DOREEN   You think she'd get a chill, wouldn't you.

                (HARRY *looks at* GARY *and* DOREEN. *He gives her the quickest of pecks and gets out of there as quickly as possible.*)

GARY   What time are we going to (*Shouting.*) party?

DOREEN   Well we don't get the Pictionary out 'til after lunch, and then it's charades and couple of games of knock-out whist.

JEAN   I think we won last year, if I'm not mistaken.

DOREEN   I think you'll find it was two all.

GARY   You're having a giraffe aren't you. I mean music and dancing and (*Shouting.*) drinking.

                (JULIE, *grabbing* HARRY, *sings and dances with him.* HARRY *tries not to enjoy it.* FRANK *returns with a drink for* JULIE.)

JULIE   I bet you've got one or two moves, haven't you?

HARRY   Well . . .

FRANK   There ya go.

                (FRANK *hands her her drink.*)

JULIE   Eee, look at the size of that. You're not wanting to get me drunk are you? (*To* HARRY, *suggestively.*) I'd hate anyone to take advantage.

                (HARRY *laughs pathetically.*)

GARY   You'll never guess what I've got for a
                Christmas present?

FRANK   (*to the audience*) Why am I not looking
                forward to this?

JULIE   It's brilliant is this.

GARY   A karaoke machine.

JULIE   He's dead good on it.

GARY   Shall I bring it over?

JULIE   He's brilliant on it.

                (GARY *bursts into song, the rest are stunned.*)

GARY   (*singing – Queen song*)
                Mama, just killed a man
                Put a gun against his head,
                Pulled a trigger now she's dead

                (GARY *continues singing.*)

JULIE   He loves Queen.

GARY   *Mama, oooh,*
                I sometimes wish I'd never been born at all.

FRANK   I think the feeling's mutual.

GARY   What?

FRANK   Carry on, carry on.

GARY   I'm gonna get it. Do you want me to get it?
                (*Singing.*) *We will, we will rock you . . .* Do
                you want me to bring it over? Right, I'll go and
                get it now, shall I?

                (*A beat.*)

JEAN   (*plucking up courage*) Maybe later, Gary.

                (*A beat, then they all join in enthusiastically.*)

FRANK	Yeah, yeah, later.
JEAN	Maybe later.
HARRY	Later sounds good.
DOREEN	Something to look forward to.
GARY	You are sure you want me to bring it over.
	(*A beat.*)
FRANK	After lunch.
JEAN	A bit later.
HARRY	Yeah.
DOREEN	(*changing the subject*) Oh Jean, you must think I'm terribly rude. I never even noticed your new carpet.
JEAN	Yeah.
GARY	I'm good on it, aren't I?
JULIE	Oh he is.
DOREEN	'Cos we've got a new carpet, you know.
JEAN	(*shocked*) Have you!
HARRY	One-and-half-K if it was a penny.
GARY	How much?
DOREEN	No change out of fifteen hundred pounds.
JEAN	(*sickened*) Really!
GARY	I could've got you a one for cheaper than that.
JULIE	Have you christened it yet?
DOREEN	I beg your pardon.

GARY	I could get you one for a lot cheaper than that.
JULIE	First thing we do isn't it.
GARY	Ask no questions.
JULIE	It's lovely and soft and spongy.
HARRY	The bloody fluff gets everywhere.
JULIE	They bloody have, the dirty buggers.
DOREEN	(*She speaks without thinking and mimics* JULIE.) We bloody haven't. (*She checks herself.*) I mean we haven't. And anyway, our Dyson soon gets rid of the fluff. Have you got a Dyson, Jean?
JEAN	No.
DOREEN	Huh!
GARY	I could get you one.
DOREEN	I don't know where I'd be without my Dyson. It picks everything up. I'm telling you, Jean, nothing sucks like a Dyson.
GARY	Our lass does.
JULIE	(*shrieking*) Eeeeee, shurrup you. What's he like?
DOREEN	(*disgusted*) I can't begin to tell you.
	(JEAN *changing the subject.*)
JEAN	(*a beat*) I tried to get Frank to go to church last night.
FRANK	(*to* HARRY) Bloody church.
HARRY	On Christmas Eve!
JEAN	I thought it might get him into the Christmas spirit.

GARY   The only church I wouldn't mind going inside
                is Charlotte.

                (*The men laugh.*)

JULIE   Eeee, what's he like? You're terrible you.
                Cheers.

ALL   Cheers.

JULIE   Oh God, I need the loo. Eee, I'm gonna wet
                meself. Oh God, it's coming.

                (*She exits back to her own house.*)

GARY   It's her condition.

FRANK   Nearly pregnant.

GARY   No, eight pints yesterday.

JEAN   We've got a loo.

GARY   Yeah, she won't go on anybody else's toilet
                she's very shy about things like that. She gets
                embarrassed. She can smell for England. Oh
                hell aye, she can shit some stuff, can Julie.

DOREEN   (*disgusted*) Well thank you for sharing that.

JEAN   Well here we are again,

FRANK   Having a good time as usual.

HARRY   Did I tell you about my new speed boat?

                (*A sense of panic hits the room as they try to
                avoid* HARRY'S *tales of canal boating.* JEAN,
                DOREEN *and* FRANK *speak simultaneously make
                their excuses and leave.*)

JEAN   I'd better check on the turkey.

DOREEN   I'll give you a hand.

FRANK   I've get the drinks.

             (*As they all exit,* HARRY'S *phone rings again.*)

HARRY   Hello. Yeah, how many more times, it's
             Christmas morning. (*He checks to see where*
             GARY *is.*) Surely you can sort that out without
             phoning me. Right. (GARY *wanders round the*
             room and as he moves upstage HARRY *talks*
             surreptitiously.) Look, I can't talk right now,
             the wife's here, for God's sake. As long as the
             hotel's booked we should be okay. Yes, I know
             the time and no, I won't . . . (FRANK *re-enters.*)
             . . . well get them out, I've already told you. I
             don't care what it costs, just do it. (*To* FRANK.)
             Sorry about that.

             (FRANK *gives* HARRY *a drink.* HARRY *puts his*
             phone down to receive it. He hands GARY *a*
             small stubby bottle of beer. GARY *holds it*
             daintily between his forefinger and his thumb.)

GARY   What the hell's that?

             (*A beat.*)

FRANK   It's a beer.

GARY   That!

FRANK   Sorry, did you want a glass?

GARY   I could shove that up me nostril.

FRANK   It's all I've got left.

GARY   What's he doing?

FRANK   Keeping an eye on his car.

GARY   Is that your car?

HARRY   Yeah.

GARY   Very nice. I like a nice car.

HARRY   30-K.

                (GARY *whistles.*)

HARRY   But it's worth it. I mean look at that rust box
                over there.

GARY   Where?

HARRY   That red one.

GARY   The Mondeo.

HARRY   Look at it! I mean you just wouldn't, would
                you.

GARY   No, you wouldn't.

HARRY   Some people don't give a damm what piece of
                junk they ride around in. Look at that heap of
                crap.

GARY   (*laughing and sharing it with* FRANK) Look at
                that heap of crap.

HARRY   What a rust bucket.

GARY   That's my car.

                (*A beat.*)

HARRY   What?

GARY   That's my car.

HARRY   Is it?

                (*Music: Jona Lewie – 'Stop the Cavalry'.*)

Scene Eight

Thirty minutes later.

FRANK   After we managed to calm him down, Gary
                eventually saw the funny side of it, before

disappearing next door to leap on his nearly pregnant wife with the hope of creating his new little boy – Tyson. I know. I never thought I'd say this but the company of Harry and Doreen seemed quite pleasing by comparison. Jean got out the hors d'oeuvres, cheese on sticks, cake, mince pies and brandy butter, oh hell aye. Well you have to don't you, it's Christmas.

(DOREEN *and* HARRY *help themselves.* FRANK *takes a mince pie and goes to eat it.*)

HARRY   Not a bad life, is it.

JEAN   Frank . . .

(He sighs deeply, puts the mince pie back and takes a bit of Christmas cake.)

FRANK   Speak for yourself.

DOREEN   Jean, you haven't got any fetish cheese have you, Jean?

JEAN   Red Leicester.

DOREEN   Not to worry. It's just we got into it last year in Greece. I can't get enough of it now, that fetish cheese. (*A beat.*) Did I mention we're buying an apartment in the south of Spain?

(JEAN *is physically shocked.*)

HARRY   120-K.

JEAN   No, no I don't think you mentioned that.

DOREEN   Just outside Torremelinos.

JEAN   (*smarting*) Well that's nice, isn't it.

FRANK   We've got a caravan in Cockermouth.

DOREEN   It's only small.

HARRY	Tiny, couldn't swing a cat round in it.
DOREEN	It's about the same size as this place.
JEAN	Well, I'm surprised you can bloody breathe if it's that small.
FRANK	Hey we could do a swap, you go to Cockermouth and we'll go to Spain.
DOREEN	I don't think so, Frank. But if the right weeks are available I'm sure you and Jean would enjoy it.
FRANK	Hey that'll be great that won't it, Jean? Off to sunny Spain.
JEAN	No thank you. I'm not that keen on Spain.
FRANK	We've been for the last ten years.
HARRY	(*enthusiastically*) And the women – (*Noticing* DOREEN.) they are not a patch on Doreen.
JEAN	You don't listen to a word I say, do you.
FRANK	I do.
JEAN	No offence, Doreen, but we've been and I don't know what it is about us and Spain, but we always end up next to some family from Grimsby, with little Ciabatta and Britney running riot. I said last year, never again, that's me and Spain finished.
DOREEN	Well the offer's still there if you change your mind. I just thought, with Crossways closing down, that beggars can't really afford to be choosers.
JEAN	Why is that then, Doreen?
DOREEN	Well it can't be easy to get another job at your age, Frank.

JEAN	I know he may not be much to look at.
FRANK	What? What do you mean I might not be much to look at?
	(ALEX *bursts through the kitchen and into the living room.*)
ALEX	Mam, Mam, we're through. We're finished! I never want to see him again.
HARRY	Who?
DOREEN	Have a day off, Harold, for God's sake.
ALEX	We were in the pub, we called for a drink and he kissed her.
FRANK	Not much to look at.
JEAN	He didn't.
ALEX	He did.
DOREEN	Well!
ALEX	I know. Auntie Jean, he kissed her. I came back from the toilet and he was kissing her.
FRANK	I think I look alright.
ALEX	Well that's it, he's buttered his bread, he can lie on it.
	(*A beat.*)
FRANK	(*to audience*) What?
ALEX	And she was common.
DOREEN	I know the type.

ALEX	She had a really, really short skirt and you could see her stocking tops peeping out.
HARRY	Really!
ALEX	And her boobs were popping out.
HARRY	Which pub was it?
DOREEN	Harry!
HARRY	'Cos we'll go and sort him out, won't we, Frank.
ALEX	Are all men like that, Mam?
DOREEN	Yes they are, pet.
HARRY	Excuse me.
DOREEN	Do you want to make her feel better?
HARRY	Yes.
DOREEN	Then shut up.
HARRY	I'm going for another drink.
	(HARRY *exits into the dining room.*)
FRANK	(*shouting after him*) Don't be shy, you help yourself.
ALEX	I wouldn't care but we were having such a good time. Only last night he was licking the nuts of my neopolitan ice cream.
FRANK	(*to the audience*) Is it me?
ALEX	Well, that's it, I've told him it's all off, I never want to see him again.
DOREEN	Here have a Ferrero Rocher?

FRANK   Is there some left? Why don't you put some in
              your pocket for later?

              (*To* FRANK'S *disgust, she does.*)

ALEX   Thanks, Uncle Frank.

FRANK   (*to the audience*) She bloody is, as well.

JEAN   I thought you were on a diet.

ALEX   I am. I'm on a diet but I'm not dyslexic or owt
              like that.

DOREEN   You stay here for dinner. Don't go round his
              parents. That's alright, isn't it, Jean.

JEAN   Not a problem, pet. You stay here with us,
              there's plenty to go round.

DOREEN   But you have to be careful, Jean, she's a
              vegetarian.

JEAN   Are you, Alex? I didn't think we'd get one of
              them in our family. Frank we've got a
              vegetarian in the family.

ALEX   But I'm a modern vegetarian, Auntie Jean.

JEAN   She's a modern one, Frank.

FRANK   What does that mean?

ALEX   I eat meat.

FRANK   (*gives a disgusted look to the audience. A
              beat*) It beggars belief, it really does.

ALEX   I'm gonna kill meself.

FRANK   Shall I get you a knife?

JEAN   Take no notice of him, he's in one of them
              moods. He's always like this when he has to
              enjoy himself.

ALEX   I was gonna give him all his Christmas presents
              back, but then I thought, why should I? Why
              should I give him the pleasure!

DOREEN   Exactly.

HARRY   (*re-entering from the dining room*) There's
              probably a simple explanation for it and
              everyone's overreacting.

ALEX   Did you know that kids were playing football
              near your car?

HARRY   The little swines. I'll bloody kill 'em.

              (*He runs out through the front door.*)

DOREEN   Well at least Richard's not an asylum seeker.

JEAN   Doreen, please.

DOREEN   It might help put things in perspective, Jean.

ALEX   A what?

DOREEN   You know Milly's run off with an asylum
              seeker.

ALEX   She hasn't.

FRANK   He's not an asylum seeker.

JEAN   Can we not talk about it?

FRANK   He's not an asylum seeker, he works with
              asylum seekers.

DOREEN   Well that's bloody worse.

FRANK   What is?

DOREEN	Encouraging 'em. Why don't they all stay in their own countries, that's what I say.
FRANK	'Cos they'll be shot or tortured.
DOREEN	So they say.
ALEX	Haven't they got their own asylums?
	(*A beat.*)
FRANK	What?
ALEX	Well if they had their own, they wouldn't have to come looking for ours.
FRANK	No, no Alex, what an asylum seeker is – oh it doesn't matter.
DOREEN	They get money for nowt. You see 'em walking round the town like they owned the country.
FRANK	Maybe we should just lock 'em in cells. Stop 'em from em going out.
DOREEN	An' they give em condoms, you know.
JEAN	Who?
DOREEN	Asylum seekers. They give 'em condoms – for nothing.
JEAN	Condoms.
DOREEN	For nothing. Not only do they give 'em money, they give em condoms.
FRANK	Well with the women round here, the poor buggers'll need all the protection they can get.
	(ALEX'S *phone rings. It is the 'Crazy Frog' ring tone.*)

ALEX	It's him. What shall I do? What shall I do?
FRANK	Why don't you answer it?
JEAN	Frank!
ALEX	Mam?
DOREEN	Answer it, darling.
ALEX	Just one minute. (*She puts her hand over the mouthpiece.*) I'll take it in the kitchen.

(ALEX *exits through into the kitchen.*)

FRANK	Harry's taking his time, isn't he? I'll go and check on him, in case he's been attacked by asylum seekers.

(FRANK *exits through the front door.*)

DOREEN	You musn't blame yourself.
JEAN	You can't help wondering. I've never met him but I've seen him through the window. And I knew he was trouble You can tell, can't you? He had that look.
DOREEN	What do you mean?
JEAN	His eyes were too close together.
DOREEN	Aha, one of them.
JEAN	And he has long hair.

(*A beat.*)

DOREEN	(*shocked*) He's not a homosexual, is he, Jean?
JEAN	I've never spoken to him. And anyway he can't be can he, if he's with our Milly.

DOREEN   Don't let that fool you for a minute. Look at
                that thing in the hairdressers, I've told 'em, I
                don't want him running his fingers – or
                anything else for that matter – through my hair.
                And he's married.

JEAN   Lets just drop it, shall we?

DOREEN   Mincing about the place. It's disgusting.

JEAN   Can we just drop it, Doreen?

DOREEN   You're right. Let's not say another word about
                it. It's enough to put you off your dinner.
                Come on, drink up. (DOREEN *switches glasses,*
                handing JEAN *hers, which is nearly empty, and*
                taking JEAN's *full glass for herself.*) We'll not
                say another word about it. (*Noticing they're*
                alone.) Harry's been gone a long time.

JEAN   He's probably having a cigarette.

DOREEN   I don't think so, Jean. He's packed in.

JEAN   Since when?

DOREEN   Since I told him he had to.

                (*They laugh.*)

JEAN   You're tough on him, Doreen.

DOREEN   He makes demands on me.

JEAN   Get away, I didn't think he dare.

DOREEN   Listen, his idea of kinky sex is doing it on a
                Tuesday – with the light on. And then about a
                month ago, I told him how much I wanted one
                of those big fridges, you know the American
                ones. Well, you know what he said to me.

JEAN   What?

DOREEN   He said he would get me one if I stopped
              wearing trousers and started wearing skirts and
              high heels a bit more.

JEAN   High heels.

DOREEN   He said heels do things for him.

JEAN   What sort of things?

DOREEN   Arouse him.

JEAN   Bloody hell.

DOREEN   Well it came last week.

              (*She waggles her foot with her high heels on.
              They laugh.*)

JEAN   I bet you did.

              (*The laugh again.*)

JEAN   You know what that makes you, don't you?

DOREEN   What?

JEAN   It's like paying for it.

DOREEN   Jean! I hope you don't think –

              (ALEX *enters, excited.*)

ALEX   Mam, Mam, he's begging me for forgiveness.
              That's good, isn't it, Mam?

DOREEN   'Course it is, pet.

ALEX   He told me the truth you see, he didn't really
              want to kiss her, And anyway she kissed him.
              He just happened to have his lips there. He's
              very honest, Auntie Jean, isn't he, Mam?

DOREEN   His dad's a teacher.

JEAN   Eee fancy that, a teacher!

DOREEN   In a private school.

ALEX   He wants me to go round. I'm in two minds
              about what to do, but they're both saying yes.
              Would you mind, Auntie Jean?

JEAN   Course not, pet.

ALEX   You're the best. Bye Auntie Jean, bye Mam.

              (She *skips out of the front room, through the
              kitchen and off.* FRANK *enters through the front
              door.*)

FRANK   (*to the audience*) Harry's put a twenty yard
              exclusion zone round his car. Now he's hiding
              in the privet to see if any kids dare to break it.

              (HARRY's *phone rings.* FRANK *picks it up and
              attempts to answer it.*)

FRANK   How the hell does this thing work?

              (*He presses buttons and inadvertently puts it
              on speaker phone.*)

FRANK   Hello?

FEMALE VOICE Hello. Can you talk yet?

FRANK   Hello?

FEMALE VOICE Right, quickly. I've confirmed the hotel and
              managed to get tickets for *Mary Poppins*, so
              I'll see you at the station at one. Don't forget –

              (FRANK *switches it off.*)

FRANK   Wrong number.

DOREEN   Don't wrong number me. Give us it here.

(*She gets the last number and phones it.*
HARRY *bursts into the room and bit of privet*
falling from his hair.)

HARRY   Bloody kids!

DOREEN   Hello.

HARRY   I'll take it.

DOREEN   Stand there. (*Into phone.*) Hello, who is this?

(*The phone goes dead.*)

DOREEN   If you want to get out of here alive, then you
               had better start talking, and start talking
               quickly.

FRANK   Would anyone like a twiglet?

DOREEN/JEAN   Shut up.

DOREEN   Well. Who was it?

HARRY   Who was what?

DOREEN   Don't come that with me. Who phoned here?
               Who are you picking up?

(HARRY, *realising the game's up, confesses.*)

HARRY   Well it's like this. I've got a meeting in
               London, to talk to a company who are thinking
               of importing our rubber seals, now, that was
               probably . . . well it's probably my secretary
               sorting out the arrangements.

DOREEN   And she's going with you, isn't she?

HARRY   Well somebody will have to take down the
               minutes.

FRANK   You dirty sod.

(*They turn and look at him.*)

FRANK   I'll just check on the turkey.

HARRY   It's business.

JEAN   It's probably something and nothing.

DOREEN   She's twenty-two.

JEAN   Oh dear.

DOREEN   And when is this little soiree supposed to be happening?

HARRY   Well . . . it's errm . . . not until . . . tomorrow.

JEAN   Tomorrow!

DOREEN   You're going away on Boxing Day?

HARRY   The meeting's on the twenty seventh. Look, it's not what you're thinking.

DOREEN   So why the big secret?

HARRY   Well it's just that . . .

JEAN   You've got something to hide.

HARRY   I haven't.

DOREEN   So why haven't you told me?

JEAN   Why haven't you told her?

HARRY   Jean, for God's sake! Look, Doreen, darling, it's like this, it's a big meeting.

DOREEN   It's that big you forgot to mention it.

HARRY   I was gonna tell you in the morning.

DOREEN   Where from, your phone on the M1?

HARRY   Look, it was a last minute thing.

DOREEN   Was it now?

HARRY   Yes. And I have to go away tomorrow, and I
          didn't think you'd understand.

DOREEN   So I'm not understanding, is that it! I'm a cold
          callous bitch, is that it?

JEAN   (*agreeing*) Well!

          (DOREEN *glares at* JEAN.)

DOREEN   (*very aggressively*) What!

JEAN   I'll just check on Frank.

HARRY   No. I mean it's understandable that you
          wouldn't understand, but if anyone was to
          understand, it would be you, because of all the
          people I know, you are the most understanding.

DOREEN   What the hell will Jean and Frank think? I'm
          humiliated. I'm so bloody humiliated. A man of
          your age and you can't control your . . . your . . .

HARRY   What?

DOREEN   Your . . . little man.

          (FRANK *enters innocently.*)

FRANK   (*innocently*) More drinks, anybody?

HARRY   Doreen, be reasonable. I have done nothing
          wrong. I am going on a business trip that
          happens to be tomorrow. I've been on
          hundreds before, and nothing happens.

          (JEAN *enters.*)

JEAN   Dinner will soon be ready.

DOREEN   Stop grovelling, you're being pathetic, you're
              starting to sound like Frank.

              (FRANK *laughs and then realises.*)

FRANK   What?

JEAN   What do you mean by that?

DOREEN   I'm sorry, Jean.

JEAN   No, come on, what do you mean by that?

DOREEN   I didn't mean anything by it, but even you
              have to admit he isn't the most dynamic man in
              the world.

JEAN   No, but he doesn't have to pay for sex.

HARRY   Paying for sex?

DOREEN   At least he's not – what? Have you been
              paying for sex?

HARRY   No.

FRANK   You dirty sod.

HARRY   Don't you start preaching to me! Have you got
              a boat?

FRANK   What?

HARRY   Have you got a boat?

FRANK   No, and you're not getting any sprouts.

DOREEN   Oh, come on, in this little council house.

JEAN   It maybe small but at least it's lived in.

DOREEN   Lived in. I think dirty's the word you're looking for.

FRANK   The hoover doesn't work.

JEAN   Frank, don't be pathetic.

DOREEN   I don't think he can help it.

JEAN   You can go to hell – and I don't mean Leeds.

DOREEN   Well come on, look at him.

FRANK   What the hell have I done?

JEAN   (*to* DOREEN) Why don't you bugger off?

DOREEN   Right –

JEAN   Fatty.

DOREEN   I've lost two pounds.

JEAN   Listen, he may not be much –

FRANK   What?

JEAN   – but he's he's kind and he's generous. And I'll tell you something else, he's . . . he's . . . well he's . . .

FRANK   Bloody hell, Jean, are you struggling.

JEAN   Shut up, Frank.

FRANK   (*to the audience*) She's bloody struggling.

JEAN   He's honest and caring and . . . that means a lot.

          (GARY, *carrying his karaoke machine, enters through the kitchen.*)

GARY   Let's get ready to rumble.

| JEAN/FRANK/ | Oh my God! |
| DOREEN/HARRY | |

(*Frosty the Snowman sings.* HARRY'S *phone rings. They all look to him.*)

HARRY   Oh shit!

(*He drops his drink all over the carpet.*)

FRANK   That's a new carpet, you daft bugger.

JEAN   Yes and it cost me two thousand pounds.

(GARY *appears together with karaoke which he triumphantly holds up in the air.*)

GARY   Party time.

HARRY   I'm sorry, Jean.

DOREEN   You will be when I get you home.

(JULIE *comes running in.*)

JULIE   Gary, Gary, the turkey's ruined.

GARY   What?

JULIE   Burnt to a cinder.

GARY   Well what the hell are we going to do for Christmas dinner now?

(*They all turn and look at* JEAN. FRANK *looks despairingly to the audience.*)

(*Music: Slade – "Well here it is Merry Christmas, Everybody's Having Fun".*)

(*Lights fade to Black.*)

ACT TWO

Scene One

As the lights come up, Slade is playing – "Here it is Merry Christmas, Everybody's having fun". They are all in the living room. GARY is stood on the arms of a chair, wearing a pirate's hat, drinking beer and singing along to Slade. He bangs an empty plastic lemonade bottle against his head. HARRY, with policeman's hat, is dancing outrageously with JULIE, who wears a pair of devil horns. JEAN, with Chinese hat, pink rubber cleaning gloves and a bucket by her side, is on her hands and knees cleaning the stain on the carpet. DOREEN sits on the settee, miserable and wearing flashing reindeer antlers. FRANK, down stage, stares out front in disbelief. Music goes down.

FRANK   Christmas has really kicked in.

                (*He puts on a paper hat.*)

                I am having loads of fun now.

                (GARY *leaps down off the chair and in a phallic gesture sticks the lemonade bottle through his legs.*)

GARY   How would you like to see the sharp end of my Jolly Roger? Ooh arr.

DOREEN   No thank you and don't be disgusting. (*She notices* HARRY.) Harry!

JULIE   (*suggestive*) He's a right good mover, aren't you, big boy?

DOREEN   (*to* HARRY) You're making a fool of yourself, I hope you realise that.

HARRY   (*deliberately teasing* DOREEN) See that? (*Showing his watch to* JULIE.) Two-and-a-half-K.

                (DOREEN *drinks her wine in one.*)

GARY   (*shouting*) Karaoke time.

> (*They all groan. Slade music up.* GARY *moves around and people pull a straw out of his hand.*)

GARY Julie (*She pulls out a straw and cheers.*) Harold. (*He pulls out a straw and cheers.*) Frankie boy. (*He pulls out a straw.*) Rudolph. Rude – olph. (DOREEN *pulls out a short straw. They all cheer. Slade music down.* GARY *chants.*) Rudolph. (JULIE *and* HARRY *join in.*) Rudolph, Rudolph, Rudolph . . .

DOREEN I don't think so.

GARY/HARRY/
JULIE (*chanting*) Rudolph, Rudolph, Rudolph . . .

FRANK (*to the audience*) People wouldn't believe this if I told 'em.

DOREEN I'm not and that's an end to it.

JEAN I thought you were a valued member of the Operatic Society.

DOREEN I am.

JEAN Well then.

DOREEN I'm head prompt.

GARY Julie gives good . . .

DOREEN DON'T! For God's sake, don't.

GARY Well prompt your way onto the karaoke, Grandma.

DOREEN I'm not a violent woman but in your case I think I'll make an exception.

JEAN This stain won't budge.

GARY Come on, it's the rules.

JULIE	It's only a laugh.
DOREEN	I don't like laughing, thank you very much.
JEAN	I think she's frightened.
GARY	(*chanting*) Frightened, frightened, frightened . . .
	(*They continue to chant under* FRANK'S *next line.*)
FRANK	(*to the audience – sarcastic*) Doesn't Christmas bring out the child in us all?
DOREEN	Right then. Give me that microphone.
	(GARY *and* JULIE *cheer.*)
GARY/JULIE	(*chanting*) Rudolph, Rudolph, Rudolph . . .
GARY	How a bit of heavy metal?
JULIE	She's too old for metal.
DOREEN	I'll have you know I'm a big fan of Bonnie Tyler.
	(GARY, JULIE *and* HARRY *laugh.* DOREEN *glares at* HARRY, *who stops instantly.*)
DOREEN	Right, if I'm to do this, I think I should do the choosing. Frank, a drink.
	(*She holds out her empty glass.*)
FRANK	Bloody hell.
	(*He gets the empty glass and disappears into the dining room to replenish it.*)
DOREEN	Have you got any Clodagh Rodgers?
JULIE	Who's Clodagh bloody Rodgers?
DOREEN	Who's Clodagh Rodgers!
GARY	We haven't got any Clodagh Rodgers. (*He switches on the Karoke machine and the intro*

to the song starts.) So you're gonna have to do a Christmas song.

DOREEN   Right then, a Christmas song it shall be.

(FRANK *re-enters with a drink for* DOREEN. *He hands it to her, she downs it one and hands the empty glass back to* FRANK.)

FRANK   *Bloody hell!*

GARY   Okay, everybody. Let's all have a warm hand on her entrance, 'cos it's the one you've all been waiting for, put your hands together for the one the only – Rudolph.

(DOREEN *snaps* GARY *a frosty look. The rest all cheer.*)

DOREEN   I'm warning you.

(DOREEN *starts to sing. It is operatic, tuneless, flat and rubbish. She misses the opening words.*)

JULIE   Come on.

DOREEN   (*singing*) . . . *Christmas every da-ay,*
Where the bells are ringing and the band begins to pla-ay . . . (*Etc.*)

(*They all join in on 'Let the bells ring out for Christmas.'*)

(*Spot on* FRANK. *The rest freeze.*)

FRANK   I bet Girls Aloud are shitting themselves. The plan was that we'd all sing a song and then we'd move on to another game. Somehow it didn't work out quite like that. One hour later we were still there.

(*Music and lights.*)

(GARY *and* JULIE *are dancing to the guitar
break from Bohemian Rhapsody.* HARRY *plays
imaginary drums.* DOREEN, *not amused, sits in
a chair.* JULIE *is chasing* HARRY *round the
room with a piece of mistletoe.* FRANK *makes
his way into the kitchen takes a huge carving
knife out of the drawer and places it, dagger
like, at his throat.* JEAN *sits stunned with her
bucket on the floor beside her.*)

GARY   Who wants another drink?

              (FRANK *runs out of the kitchen and into the
              living room.*)

FRANK   What did you say?

JULIE   I'll have a gin.

GARY   (*to* JULIE) You're not having gin. When she has
              Gin she always gets her tits out.

JULIE   Shurrup you. I do like.

DOREEN   Oh please.

HARRY   Yes please.

              (DOREEN *glares at him.*)

JULIE   Are you taking advantage of me? Gary, he's
              taking advantage of me.

GARY   (*serious*) Hey you.

HARRY   (*panicking*) I'm not. Honest, I wouldn't do that.

GARY   (*singing*) *Get Off My Cloud. Hey, hey, you,
              you get off of my cloud. Hey you . . .* (*Slapping*
              FRANK'*s face in time to the beat.*) . . . get the
              drinks in.

              (GARY *continues to sing.*)

FRANK   I don't think there's any left. I think we've
                 drank it all. What a shame we'll all have to go
                 home.

GARY   (*still singing*) There's bloody loads out there.
                 (*Stops singing.*) Anybody else want one?

DOREEN   I'll have a large one.

GARY   I bet you will, you randy old sod. Harry, get the
                 drinks in.

FRANK   (*looking up to heaven*) Please don't do this to
                 me. I'll be good. I promise.

                 (HARRY, *like a lap dog, goes into the dining
                 room to get the drinks.* JULIE *follows.*)

FRANK   (*to the audience*) It's my bloody house. Gary
                 has taken over. My bloody house. I'm gonna
                 bloody hit him in a minute.

JEAN   (*aside to* FRANK *and with bucket in hand.*)
                 They're going mad. They're pouring the drinks
                 down them.

FRANK   Well, it's Christmas.

JEAN   You're pathetic.

DOREEN   (*pissed*) Where's my drink?

FRANK   She's pissed. Do something.

JEAN   You do something, I'm trying to clean the carpet.

FRANK   She's your sister.

                 (HARRY *comes bursting out of the dining room
                 carrying drinks all flustered and dishevelled,
                 quickly followed by* JULIE. JEAN *takes the
                 bucket into the kitchen.*)

HARRY   (*pathetically whimpers out a plea for help*)
                 Calm down.

JULIE	What!
HARRY	Calm down.
GARY	Right, that's it.

(*The room goes quiet.* HARRY *freezes like a rabbit in the headlights.*)

I need a gypsy's kiss.

(*They all breathe a sigh of relief.*)

DOREEN	A what?
GARY	I'm just gonna syphon the python, But don't go away, I'll be back.

(GARY *exits to the toilet.*)

FRANK	That's someat to look forward to then.
DOREEN	Right, I'll get my own drink.

(DOREEN *disappears into the dining room.*)

JEAN	(*head popping out of the kitchen door*) Frank, can I have a word?

(FRANK *disappears into the kitchen.* JULIE *approaches* HARRY.)

JULIE	Are you avoiding me?
HARRY	No. I think you're very nice.
JULIE	Lets have a dance.
HARRY	No! Let's chat! So what did you get for Christmas?

(JULIE *unzips the front of her dress.*)

JULIE	These.

HARRY   What?

JULIE   Me boobs. I've had a boob job. Gary loves 'em.
          What do you think?

HARRY   Well. They're . . . err . . . very nice.

JULIE   Can you tell they're false?

HARRY   No.

JULIE   Squeeze 'em.

          (*A beat.*)

HARRY   What?

JULIE   Squeeze 'em. Tell me what you think.

          (HARRY *half laughs pathetically.*)

HARRY   Squeeze 'em, right . . .

JULIE   How do they feel?

HARRY   (*not believing his luck, he is in a state of
          euphoric ecstasy*) Bloody gorgeous.

          (DOREEN *enters the living room.*)

JULIE   Jiggle 'em up and down.

HARRY   Right.

DOREEN   What the hell is going on?

HARRY   You're not gonna believe this.

DOREEN   I'm know I'm not.

JULIE   He was just jiggling me boobs.

HARRY   (*laughing and making light of it*) It was her
          Christmas present.

DOREEN   It was her Christmas present, was it? Right, I
          think I'll be giving you yours any minute.

GARY   (*from off, shouts*) Julie, Julie, Julie, come here a
                minute.

JULIE   (*shrieking*) What do you want?

DOREEN   (*ringing out her ear*) And which finishing
                school did you go to?

JULIE   What? I'll have to go, his master has called.
                (*Shouting.*) I'm coming. (*Chuntering as she
                exits.*) He's gonna get it when I go upstairs.

DOREEN   What the hell do you think you're doing?

HARRY   What do you mean?

DOREEN   Don't come that with me. You've been glaring
                at that woman's . . . chest all through dinner.

HARRY   I'm sure I haven't.

DOREEN   You've been staring at them.

HARRY   I haven't.

DOREEN   You have.

HARRY   I couldn't help it, they were poking me in the eye.

DOREEN   But that wasn't enough was it, you've had to
                have your hands all over 'em. You're a pervert.

HARRY   She wanted me to.

DOREEN   Oh well, that's alright then, as long as she
                consented.

Harrry   No, you don't understand –

DOREEN   You're doing it on purpose. You want me to be
                humiliated.

HARRY   I don't.

DOREEN   If it isn't one hussy it's another.

HARRY	Look, how many times –
DOREEN	I don't know how many times. I wish I did.
HARRY	I could bloody scream, I could. I'm going for a drink.

(He exits into the dining room. DOREEN follows.)

DOREEN	Don't you walk away from me.

(FRANK and JEAN are in the kitchen.)

JEAN	I don't care, you're gonna have to do something, they've ruined me bloody carpet.
FRANK	You bloody invited 'em.
JEAN	Well you'll have to get rid of them.
FRANK	How?
JEAN	I don't know.

(JEAN exits into the lounge.)

FRANK	Well what do you want me to do, shit a solution?

(FRANK follows her into the lounge.)

JEAN	Where is everybody?
FRANK	Maybe all my prayers have been answered. Look, she's your bloody sister.
JEAN	You're the man of the house.
FRANK	Oh, not that old chestnut.
JEAN	Where are they?
FRANK	Well I hope she's bloody buggered off, 'cos I can't stand the snobby cow.

(HARRY *enters from the dining room.*)

HARRY   Bugger off.

(DOREEN *comes belting in after him.*)

DOREEN   Come back here you . . . Jean, Frank, hi.

FRANK   Hello Doreen, we've just been wondering
             where you were. We were getting worried. Oh,
             you're getting a drink, that is good, isn't it.
             We like it when people help themselves to our
             drink, don't we, Jean?

             (*At that we hear the creaking of a bed and the
             knocking of a headboard on a wall coming
             from above.*)

             What the hell's that?

JEAN   I think it's next door.

HARRY   Is it coming from upstairs?

             (*They all stop and listen. Simultaneously they
             all slowly look up at the ceiling.*)

FRANK   It sounds like . . .

JEAN   It does, doesn't it. I don't believe it.

             (*They here some wailing and screaming
             coming from upstairs.* JULIE *and* GARY *are
             bonking.*)

JULIE   (*off*) Oh my God! Oh my God! Yes! Yes!

GARY   (*off*) Come on, come on, come on.

             (*Grinding and wailing happens under all the
             next dialogue.*)

FRANK   It's Julie and Gary.

DOREEN   (*innocently*) What are they doing?

HARRY	Well I don't think it's Pictionary.
FRANK	Not a bloody gen.
JEAN	You'll have to stop them, Frank.
FRANK	What?
JEAN	They're in our bed.
FRANK	I know.
JEAN	Well do something.
FRANK	What do you want me to do?
DOREEN	It's outrageous.
JEAN	(*a sudden thought*) I hope you picked your underpants up off the floor.
	(*A beat.*)
FRANK	(*aghast*) What?
JEAN	I hope you've left that bedroom nice and tidy.
FRANK	They are bonking in our bed and you're worried about my bloody underpants.
JEAN	I don't want your shitty underpants lying all over the place.
FRANK	They're doing it in our bed. Listen to 'em. They're gonna come through the ceiling. They're gonna come through the bloody ceiling.
HARRY	How do they keep it going for so long?
DOREEN	Well that's a mystery I don't think you'll ever solve.
JULIE	(*off, screaming*) Aaaaah. Aaaah.

GARY   (*off*) Oh yes. Oh yes. Oh Yes. (*He has a few
                final grunts before on long final exclamation.*)
                Yeee . . . eeee . . . eeee . . . ssssss. It's a kind of
                magic.

FRANK   (*to* JEAN) You'll have to stop 'em.

JEAN   I will? I can't bear to listen. It's too much. I'm
                gonna have another go at that stain.

                (*She exits to the kitchen for a cloth.*)

DOREEN   (*to* HARRY) Look at you, you wish it was you,
                don't you.

HARRY   No.

DOREEN   You do. What I don't understand is how you
                go chasing after women when you've got me at
                home.

FRANK   You know, you're right there, Doreen.

HARRY   For God's sake shut up.

DOREEN   Oh but he's right.

JEAN   (*coming out of the kitchen with a cloth and
                approaching the stain*) Frank, get me some
                white wine, that might shift it.

                (FRANK *goes to the dining room.*)

DOREEN   And as for paying for sex?

HARRY   I haven't.

DOREEN   Huh!

HARRY   Don't you 'huh' me, 'cos the only time I've
                paid for sex was when I met you.

DOREEN   I'll not have that kind of talk, do you hear me?

HARRY   You think everyone's as wicked as you.

DOREEN   How dare you!

                (FRANK *re-enters with a glass of white wine.*)

HARRY   At least I haven't let myself go.

FRANK/JEAN   (*gasp*) Ooh!

DOREEN   Well you've . . . you've got a face like . . . a . . .
                like a . . . pair of tits – and that's swearing.

HARRY   Well at least that's one decent pair in our
                relationship.

                (*A beat.* FRANK *inadvertently sets the karaoke
                machine into action.*)

DOREEN   You'll pay for that last remark.

                (*She starts to attack him with a cushion. The
                up stage door burst open and* GARY *enters,
                stands and poses. He pushes a hoover. He has
                baubles off the tree for earrings,* JEAN'S *shower
                cap, and* JULIE'S *skirt, high heels and one of*
                JEAN'S *bras on. He also sports a 'Freddie
                Mercury' type moustache. He sings along to
                the karaoke.*)

GARY   *I want to break free. I want to break from this
                life . . . (Etc.)*

                (MILLY *enters the kitchen and hesitates.*)

DOREEN   (*to* GARY) Shut up. Just shut that infernal
                machine off.

                (GARY *stops singing.*)

GARY   What?

DOREEN   Off, get the bloody thing off. I can't hear
                myself think.

                (GARY *switches the machine off.*)

GARY	Listen wobble gob, nobody speaks to me like that.
DOREEN	Well I do. Do you hear me? I do.
GARY	What?

(FRANK *leaps in between them and ushers* GARY *to the side.*)

FRANK	Gary, please, she's not well.
HARRY	(*defiantly*) I liked your singing, Gary.
DOREEN	(*whacks him one with the cushion*) You speak when you're spoken to. (*She continues to hit him with the cushion.*) How dare you! How dare you go lusting after other women. You pig. I hate you, you pig. Christmas present, I'll give you a Christmas present.
FRANK	(*trying to lighten the situation*) Shall I get the Pictionary out now?
DOREEN	I've looked after you like a bloody mother. We're through, do you hear me?

(FRANK *points his forefinger at his head, implying she's a little mad.* GARY *acknowledges him.*)

JEAN	Where's that white wine?
GARY	I'll put us another song on.
FRANK/JEAN	No!

(MILLY *enters the lounge.*)

GARY	(*angry*) What do you mean, 'no'!
FRANK	We mean yes – but a bit later. Errr, Jean wants to use your strength to help get this stain out of the carpet, don't you.
JEAN	Yeah, that's right.

GARY   Well why didn't you say?

FRANK   (*to the audience, relieved that he's got himself
                out of a bit of a predicament*) Bloody hell! Oh
                here's the white wine.

                (GARY *takes it and drinks it.* DOREEN *is still
                battering* HARRY.)

JEAN   It's for the carpet, you daft bugger.

MILLY   The door was open.

                (*Everybody stops and turns towards* MILLY,
                except GARY, *who is hell bent on removing the
                stain.*)

JEAN   (*stunned*) Oh my God!

DOREEN   Well this is a turn up for the books.

MILLY   Hello, Auntie Doreen.

GARY   (*referring to the stain*) It's nearly out.

HARRY   Have you seen my car out front?

FRANK   Can I get you a drink? I don't think there's any
                Buck's Fizz left, some buggers drank it all. But
                we do have one bottle of Blossom Hill, I'm sure
                there'll be enough for one glass each.

MILLY   I'm not that bothered.

DOREEN   We know that.

HARRY   Will you butt out?

DOREEN   Right you, outside.

HARRY   Well I don't think –

DOREEN   Now! We have a number of things that need
                discussing.

HARRY   (*exiting*) I've been to a lap dancing club but
              that doesn't, count does it, and I only went the
              once.

              (DOREEN *marches out and takes a Ferrero
              Rocher as she goes.*)

GARY   Hey Harry, next time you're going, give us a
              knock will you? (*To* FRANK.) What's the matter
              with your lass? Did someone drop her on her
              head when she was a kid?

FRANK   This is Milly.

GARY   Hello, I'm Gary. I live next door. I've got a
              karaoke for Christmas.

              (*He shakes her hand. Music: In Dulce Jubilo
              – Mike Oldfield. Minutes later . . .*)

FRANK   Gary retrieved Julie who'd collapsed on our
              bed and carried her home. Doreen, get this,
              came in and took a bottle of my bloody wine
              back outside. I could bloody scream, I could.
              But one good thing, Milly was back. Jean was
              struck dumb. She didn't know what to say. The
              two of them just stood there looking at each
              other.

              Well this is nice, isn't it? (*A beat.*) It's a nice
              surprise, isn't it? (*A beat.*) You, me and your
              Mam. (*A beat.*) The three of us. It's jusk like
              old times. (*A beat. To the audience.*) Oh shit!

MILLY   How've you been?

JEAN   (*defiantly*) Brilliant.

              (FRANK, *as ever, tries to lighten the tension.*)

FRANK   If you want a Ferrero Rocher I'd get in now.

(*A pause. They force embarrassed smiles at
each other. The atmosphere is very strained.
Pause.*)

JEAN   Where have you been living?

MILLY   I've bought a flat in Marton.

JEAN   You've bought a flat?

MILLY   In Marton.

JEAN   But how can you afford . . .

MILLY   Look, I'm working an that, alright?

           (*A beat.*)

JEAN   Is it with . . . you know.

FRANK   Darren. His name's Darren. Just say it, for
           God's sake.

           (*A beat.*)

JEAN   Have you?

MILLY   I haven't come here for an argument.

JEAN   Do you know how upset I have been? I've been
           worried sick.

MILLY   I'm sorry.

FRANK   Well that's alright. If she's sorry. You're sorry,
           we're sorry, everybody's sorry. That's okay
           then. Shall we have a cup of tea and a mince
           pie?

JEAN   You have put me through hell!

MILLY   Do you think it was easy for me? Do you think
           I enjoyed it?

JEAN   Your trouble is you're just like your father.

FRANK   What?

JEAN   I've been too soft with you. I should have been firmer.

MILLY   I'm going.

JEAN   And then you wouldn't have run off with *him*.

MILLY   Darren. His name's Darren.

JEAN   I don't care what the hell his name was –

MILLY   Is, mother, is.

         (FRANK *snaps*.)

FRANK   (*shouting*) Right, that's it. Just shut up for one minute. Just bloody keep quiet. (*Calming*.) I am fed up with this. I'm fed up to the back teeth of the bloody lot of it. I daren't speak. It's like walking on broken glass round here. You left home because of her –

JEAN   Me!

FRANK   Shut up. All your problems were with your mother. That's it, isn't it. That's why you stormed out. But what about me? Who gave me any thought?

MILLY   I didn't do it to have . . .

FRANK   Shut up! I'll tell you who gave me some thought. Nobody. Nobody ever considers how I feel or what I think. I'm just expected to get on. Well let me tell you, this isn't easy for me. I've lost my job. Doreen thinks I'm pathetic and Jean struggles to say anything good about me. (*To* MILLY.) I didn't want you to go. I wanted you to stay. For God's sake, you're my little girl. (*Turning with anger to* JEAN, *who, shocked, jumps*.) And you! What the hell do you want? She's here. She's home. That's all

you've ever wanted so what the hell is the
matter with you? Pride comes before a fall,
Jean. So I'm warning you now, don't blow this.
Got it? Right I'm gonna take the dog for a walk.

(*Silence.*)

MILLY   I know I've been a disappointment to you.

JEAN   You haven't.

MILLY   Oh come on, mam, let's just be honest with
            each other for once. I'm not the person you
            wanted me to be.

JEAN   You were alright until you met him.

MILLY   That's not true and you know it's not.

            (*A beat.*)

JEAN   He dragged you away from me.

MILLY   Look let's get this clear once and for all. This
            has got nothing to do with Darren. Everything I
            did, right or wrong, was down to me. I made
            that decision. When I walked out of that front
            door all I wanted to do was wipe that smug, 'I
            know better', smile off your face. And then the
            longer I was away, the more difficult it was to
            come back. I wanted to, but I couldn't. I
            wanted to prove to you that I could do it on my
            own. That I don't need you. That I'm not a
            failure.

JEAN   You're not. You're not a failure and you didn't
            have to prove anything.

MILLY   Yeah I know. I know that now.

JEAN   So why now? Why come back now?

            (*A beat.*)

MILLY

I dunno. (*A beat.*) Well, it's Christmas isn't it, and I've never spent a Christmas away from home. (*A beat.*) And I missed you. And my three-legged cow.

(*A beat. HARRY comes marching through the kitchen and back into the living room. DOREEN is in hot pursuit. She carries a wine glass in one hand and a bottle of wine in the other.*)

DOREEN

Come back here, do you hear me?

HARRY

Bugger off!

(*HARRY marches out.*)

DOREEN

I'm warning you, you walk out that door and we're through, do you hear me? Through. (*The door slams. Screaming after him.*) Bastard! And that's swearing.

(*She has consumed more alcohol than she is used to. She looks at the glass and thinks, 'to hell with it' and drinks copious amounts out of the bottle.*)

He's gone. Did you see that? I'm sorry, Milly, but do you see what I have to put up with? He's walked out on me. He's said he's going to the pub until I calm down. I mean, calm down. I am calm. (*Screaming.*) Do I look not calm? Calm! How the hell dare he? Season of Goodwill! Right, I am going to chop his bloody balls off. I am. And I'm gonna put 'em in a jar and stick 'em on the mantelpiece.

JEAN

Have a drink, come on, calm down.

(*JEAN pours her a drink. There is a ring at the door.*)

DOREEN

That'll be him. (*She necks her drink in one.*) Get me a knife, and make sure it's a big bugger.

JEAN	Calm down, Doreen.

MILLY	I'll get the door.

DOREEN   (*shouting after her*) Tell him to go and die. If
           he thinks he can walk back in here, he's got
           another thing coming. How do I look?

JEAN   You look fine.

MILLY   Mum there's someone I'd like you to meet.
           Darren's here.

DOREEN   Darren?

JEAN   He's here.

MILLY   He wants to meet you. Please.

           (*A beat.*)

JEAN   Well you'd better bring him in.

           (MILLY *exits.*)

DOREEN   Some people don't care who they upset. Don't
           you worry your head on his account, leave this
           to me, I'll sort the bugger out.

           (JEAN *and* DOREEN *sit on the settee.* DARREN
           enters, along with MILLY. *He has a pony tail
           but is generally quite smart, though somewhat
           distinct.*)

DOREEN   (*under her breath*) Look at his eyes.

MILLY   Darren this is my mum, Jean, Mum, this is Darren.

           (DARREN *is hesitant.*)

           Well go on then.

           (*He moves toward her and shakes her hand. At
           the same time* DOREEN *evasively moves away.*)

DARREN   Pleased to meet you, Mrs Bailey.

MILLY   Jean.

                (DARREN *is a bit nervous. He looks to* MILLY
                for help. Impatiently she eggs him on.)

DARREN   Jean.

MILLY   And this is my Auntie Doreen, she's me mam's
                sister.

DOREEN   Younger sister, actually.

MILLY   She's lovely really.

                (DOREEN, *a formidable figure, glowers in his
                direction.*)

DARREN   How do you do?

                (DOREEN, *glowering, offers no reaction. He
                offers to shake her hand. She refuses.*)

MILLY   Take your coat off.

DARREN   I'm fine.

MILLY   Take your coat off.

                (DARREN *hesitantly removes his coat to reveal
                another hideous jumper, like* FRANK'S. *Pause.*)

DARREN   Christmas present.

                (*He half-laughs, but realising that he is
                getting no reaction from* JEAN *or* DOREEN *he
                stops, embarrassed. Pause.*)

MILLY   Would you like a drink?

DARREN   I could kill for a beer.

DOREEN   Yes, I bet you could.

MILLY	You'll have an orange juice, you're driving. What's he like? He'll have an orange juice. (*A beat.*) Right, I'll get it then, shall I? Is it . . .
JEAN	Dining room.
	(MILLY *exits.* DARREN *looks after her for support – she is gone. He feels vulnerable. A pause. They look at each other.*)
DOREEN	I suppose you think you're clever, turning a young girl's head.
JEAN	(*embarrassed at the severity of* DOREEN'S *attack*) Doreen!
DARREN	What?
DOREEN	Don't come that with me 'cos it doesn't wash. And neither do you, by the looks of things.
DARREN	Sorry?
DOREEN	I've met your sort before. Are you, or are you not . . . cohabiting?
DARREN	No, no. You've got it wrong.
DOREEN	No, I think it's you that's got it wrong, Tonto.
JEAN	Doreen!
DARREN	No, I don't live with Milly, if that's what you're thinking. Milly lives on her own. She's buying her own flat. She won't live with anyone until she's married. She says her mother wouldn't approve.
JEAN	Is that what she said?
	(*A beat.* MILLY *pops her head round the door.*)
MILLY	(*handing* DARREN *his juice*) There you go.

DARREN   Thanks.

DOREEN   I hear you work with asylum seekers.

DARREN   Yeah.

DOREEN   Do you give 'em condoms?

DARREN   What?

DOREEN   You heard, do you give 'em condoms?

DARREN   Not personally, no.

JEAN   Doreen!

MILLY   He has some really sad tales to tell.

DOREEN   Don't we all.

MILLY   (*to* DARREN) Go on, tell 'em what happened last
                week.

DARREN   Shurrup.

MILLY   It's tragic.

DOREEN   You don't have to tell me, I know it bloody is.

MILLY   No It's about this guy, he had his house
                destroyed, and then he had to flee his country,
                leaving his family behind. He's been round this
                morning taking Christmas presents for him
                haven't you?

DARREN   It was nowt, just a few little things.

DOREEN   And who's paying for the presents, that's what
                I want to know.

MILLY   He does. It's his own money, he thinks he's
                Bob Geldof.

JEAN   That's very nice of him, isn't it, Doreen? You
                know, caring for others.

DARREN	Nice house.
JEAN	Do you think?
DOREEN	I think it's a bit small.
DARREN	I think it's warm and cosy.
JEAN	It's a bit of a mess at the moment. I'm embarrassed. We've been invaded.
DARREN	Neighbours and family.
DOREEN	I'll have you know I've only had two glasses of wine.
DARREN	Course you have. (*To* JEAN.) Don't worry, it's the same at our house.
DOREEN	And I was invited.
DARREN	(*noticing the tree*) Nice tree. I hate those fancy co-ordinated ones, don't you?
JEAN	(*enjoying it*) I can't think of anything worse.
DARREN	Thank God it isn't a real one.
DOREEN	(*sarcastically*) Oh, perish the thought. And where do you live?
MILLY	Little Lord Darren lives with his parents over at Nunthorpe, don't ya. He went to the private school there.
DARREN	Shurrup.
JEAN	Did you hear that, Doreen? He went to a private school. What am I thinking, would you like a bit of Christmas cake? (*Before he has chance to answer.*) Course you would. With a bit of cheese and some brandy butter no doubt. I bet you have brandy butter at Nunthorpe. Or would you like a Marks and Spencer's mince pie?

DARREN   Cake would be fine.

JEAN   I'll bring both and you know why? 'Cos I can.

MILLY   I'll give you a hand.

              (*They exit.* DOREEN *and* DARREN *are alone.
              There is an embarrassed silence,* DOREEN
              feeling very uncomfortable.)

DOREEN   I'll tell you this for nowt. I don't like
              homosexuals, I never have done and I never will.

              (DARREN *looks over both shoulders, imagining
              that she must be talking to someone else. She
              storms out.* FRANK *enters.*)

FRANK   (*he turns and sees* DARREN – *he jumps a bloody
              mile. He adopts a karate pose.*) Who the fuck
              are you?

DARREN   You must be Milly's dad?

FRANK   I know who I am but who the fuck . . . are you?

DARREN   I'm Darren, Milly's boyfriend?

FRANK   Oh, bloody hell. Sorry about that but you can't
              be too careful these days. I'm Frank.

DARREN   Yeah, I recognised the top.

FRANK   The bloody women in this family.

              (*An awkward pause.*)

DARREN   They've gone to get some cake.

FRANK   Oh hell, I'm warning you now, it's bloody
              awful. It's her pride and joy but it's bloody
              awful. If you don't want to spend Boxing Day
              on the toilet, take my advice and go for the
              mince pies.

	(*The women re-enter.* DOREEN *carefully gives* DARREN *evasive action.*)
JEAN	Here we are, Christmas cake.
DARREN	I think I'd rather have a mince pie, if you don't mind.
FRANK	What? (*Stepping back in amazement*). I can't believe you've just said that. Turning down some of Jean's cake!
JEAN	My cake does have a reputation for being lovely and moist.
	(*Everybody turns to look at* JEAN.)
FRANK	(*to the audience*) Don't.
DARREN	I really like mince pies.
JEAN	I'll tell you what, you can have his bit, Frank.
	(FRANK *panics*.)
FRANK	What! NO! (*A beat.*) Well . . . err . . . I'd love some but I'm stuffed after that gorgeous dinner, (*A piece of inspiration.*) and I want to . . . er, to try and make it last.
JEAN	I thought you might change your mind, Darren, once you'd seen them. I think I mentioned they were from Marksies, didn't I? We get all our food from Marksies.(*A beat.*) Well, this is nice, isn't it. Are you staying for tea . . . Darren?
	(MILLY *smiles.* FRANK *is shocked.* JEAN *has got his name right.*)
FRANK	(*to the audience*) Darren.
DOREEN	Tea!
MILLY	Darren's got something to ask you, haven't you, Darren?

(DARREN *panics and chokes on the pie.*)

DARREN   Have I?

DOREEN   I bloody knew it! I told you, didn't I? Didn't I tell you?

MILLY   Go on. (*Encouraging him.*) Their present.

(DARREN *breathes a sigh of relief.*)

DARREN   Oh yes. Oh right.

MILLY   Well it's like this, we'd booked to go to his parents' villa in Tenerife.

DOREEN   Our villa's in Spain.

DARREN   Well, what it is, I'm working, at Easter, so we can't go, and we'd like you and Frank to have our two weeks, wouldn't we?

MILLY   Yeah.

JEAN   Well that would be lovely. Oh thank you. Have you ever been to Tenerife, Doreen?

DOREEN   You know that's one place I've never wanted to go.

JEAN   But we haven't got you anything.

FRANK   If we'd known you were coming we could have got you some shampoo or something.

MILLY   Dad!

FRANK   What?

DARREN   Well look, I must dash, mother gets herself in a flap if I'm late.

MILLY   I'm just gonna nip to Darren's to see his mum
               and dad and give them their present, but don't
               worry, I'm coming back. I won't be long.

DARREN   Happy Christmas.

               (FRANK and JEAN wish him 'Happy Christmas'
               and DARREN and MILLY exit through the front
               door.)

JEAN   What a nice young man.

DOREEN   Oh come on.

FRANK   Tenerife. Bloody Tenerife.

JEAN   When was it again?

FRANK   Easter.

JEAN   Tenerife at Easter. I've never been to Tenerife.

DOREEN   Very windy I hear, and it's got black sand.

FRANK   Sounds a big place.

JEAN   Not like this poky little hole.

FRANK   No, not like this.

DOREEN   You can visit but it isn't yours, is it. You can
               have two weeks but then you have to give it
               back, so before you start gloating too much I
               think you should remember that little fact. You
               haven't got a villa, you haven't got a boat, so
               you tell me what exactly have you got?

JEAN   We've got a fortnight.

FRANK   In Tenerife.

JEAN   At Easter.

DOREEN   It's bribery. It's probably all drug money.

FRANK   (singing to the "La Conga" tune) Tenerife at
               Easter, Tenerife at Easter, da da da da . . .

(FRANK *picks up a mince pie and on the last da, victoriously pops it in his mouth.*)

DOREEN   And to be honest I think this cake's a bit dry. I need a drink. (*Sarcastically.*) You don't mind, do you, Frank?

FRANK   (*speaking with his mouthful*) Help yourself.

(DOREEN *goes up to the dining room to get a drink.*)

JEAN   What are you eating?

(FRANK *is shocked and freezes like a rabbit in the headlights.*)

JEAN   You're eating a mince pie, aren't you?

(FRANK *shakes his head. His mouth is obviously full.*)

JEAN   I've just seen you.

FRANK   (*putting his hand over his mouth, and speaking with his mouthful*) It's a piece of cake.

JEAN   You're eating a Marks and Spencer's mince pie.

FRANK   I'm not.

JEAN   I've only bought a dozen.

FRANK   It's cake.

JEAN   What have I told you?

FRANK   It's a piece of bloody cake.

(ALEX *enters through the kitchen.*)

ALEX   Mam, Mam . . . Auntie Jean.

JEAN   What is it, pet?

ALEX	Me dad came in the pub and he's pouring them down his neck.
JEAN	I think he's a little upset.
ALEX	He threatened to chop me mam's head off.
JEAN	I'm sure he didn't mean it.

(DOREEN *appears with another drink. She totters slightly.*)

ALEX	Mam, you have to get out of here, Dad's going to decaffeinate you.
DOREEN	What?
ALEX	And then he's going to bury you under the patio.
DOREEN	He is, is he?
ALEX	I've never seen him like this before. He threw his hands up said, Happy Birthday Jesus and then ordered a Multiple Orgasm.
JEAN	What's a Multiple Orgasm?
DOREEN	Exactly.
ALEX	He said, he wanted to say he'd had at least one before the year's out. Oh, it was so embarrassing. I started talking to Nai.
FRANK	Who's Nai?
ALEX	She's my friend?
FRANK	What's Nai short for?
ALEX	She's got little legs.

(*A beat.*)

FRANK	I need a drink.

ALEX   I didn't know where to put myself. And then
              he started calling Richard Dick and making all
              kinds of coarse dick jokes, What're we gonna
              do?

DOREEN   Leave your father to me, I can handle your
              father.

ALEX   But Mam –

DOREEN   He did this when he turned forty, he stopped
              wearing socks and started listening to Radio
              One.

ALEX   I sneaked out and ran ahead to warn you.

JEAN   What're you gonna do with him, Doreen?

DOREEN   I don't know. I really don't. I'm at the end of
              my rope.

FRANK   (*to audience*) Now there's a pleasant thought.

ALEX   He's coming here now.

DOREEN   Just act normal.

FRANK   Well that's a bloody challenge.

DOREEN   Was your father singing?

ALEX   No.

DOREEN   Oh well, as long as he isn't singing we've got a
              chance.

HARRY   (*singing, off*) *So here it is Happy Christmas* . . .

DOREEN   Oh hell. Quick, you go and apologise to Richard.

ALEX   But Mam . . .

DOREEN   Go.

HARRY   (*off*) *Look to the future now, it's only just beguuuuuu . . . uuu . . . un . . .*

DOREEN   You've been drinking.

(HARRY *takes out a cigarette and puts it in his mouth.*)

What are you doing?

HARRY   I am having a cigarette. A bloody gorgeous soon-to-be-banned-off-the-planet cigarette.

(*He takes out a lighter and flicks it with his thumb. The flame is huge and nearly sets his whole face alight.*)

Oh bloody hell.

(*He carefully lights the cigarette and takes delight in having a drag and exhaling the smoke.*)

DOREEN   Put that out. I order you to put that out immediately.

(HARRY *defiantly puffs it a few times straight at her.*)

I'm sorry about this, Jean. (*To* HARRY.) You do this every year, you get too much to drink. You might be big and clever here but by hell wait till I get you home.

HARRY   (*raising his voice*) Shut your big fat mouth.

(*He stamps his foot. Santa bursts into life, singing "Jingle Bells".*)

FRANK   It does that.

(FRANK *claps his hands, nothing happens.*)

DOREEN   For God's sake.

(*She claps her hands and it stops.*)

FRANK   (*to the audience*) I'm bloody sick of this.

JEAN   I'm gonna check on the turkey.

FRANK   (*to the audience*) We've already had lunch.

             (*She exits.*)

HARRY   You're gonna listen to me for a change. You
             can decide whether or not I go to the meeting.

             (DOREEN *goes to speak.* HARRY *cuts her off.*)

             But before you put that mouth of yours into
             overdrive, I want you to be aware of some
             facts. One, we are skint.

FRANK   (*shouting*) Jean, come and listen to this.

             (DOREEN *glares at* FRANK.)

             Sorry, Doreen.

DOREEN   (*to* HARRY) You're drunk. (*She hiccups.*)

HARRY   I've had a drink, but I'm definitely not drunk.

             (JEAN *enters.*)

FRANK   (*to* JEAN) They're skint.

JEAN   What?

DOREEN   Take no notice of him.

FRANK   They've got no bloody 'K'.

HARRY   Correct. We are in real danger of losing the
             business. And if we lose the business, we lose
             the house. And – the car.

FRANK   What about the boat?

HARRY   We lose the boat.

FRANK	Thank God for that.
HARRY	Our Alex's car will have to go back.
DOREEN	(*aghast*) That was her Christmas present.
HARRY	But we ain't paid for it. And this meeting, is a little bit of a last throw of the dice. So what is it to be? Do you want me to go?
FRANK	You could always come with us to Tenerife.
DOREEN	You're lying, he's lying.
HARRY	Right, lets ring Lesley. My secretary who is very beautiful.
FRANK	So's Doreen.
DOREEN	Shut up, Frank!
HARRY	I'll tell you what, better still, lets go round to her house. She has been frantically talking to these Americans, and on Christmas Day as well. How devoted is that – working on Christmas Day. Can you remember what work is? And you call her, you jealous bugger. You're even jealous of your own sister.
FRANK	She's jealous of you.
JEAN	Are you?
DOREEN	How could I be jealous of her?
JEAN	You what?
HARRY	The only reason you got a new carpet was 'cos you heard Jean had got one.
DOREEN	You're a liar. I didn't, honest, he's making it up.
HARRY	You were like a rat up a drain pipe, you couldn't get into town quick enough.
JEAN	Me own bloody sister.

DOREEN   Don't listen to him.

JEAN   You can see me with nowt.

GARY   (*entering through the kitchen*) Party time.

                (*He switches off the light and then with torch
                in hand shining on his face and on others he
                sings.*)

                *I see a little silhouetto of a man,
                Scaramouche, scaramouche will you do the
                fandango,
                Thunderbolt and lightning – Doreen's very
                frightening me
                Galileo, Galileo,
                Galileo, Galileo,
                Galileo Figaro – magnifico . . .*

                (FRANK *switches on the light.*)

FRANK   Gary, it's good to see you've come back.

GARY   Doreen, you're an attractive woman. If I was
                thirty years older I could go for you.

FRANK   What with, a carving knife?

HARRY   So about the meeting, what is it to be?
                (*Singing and mimicking* GARY.) *Should I go or
                should I stay?*

GARY   No, stay, there's a party over at Sheila's.

                (DOREEN *is upset.*)

DOREEN   Why are you doing this to me? After all I've
                done for you. I'm sorry, Jean. I'm not staying
                here with this pig any more. Thanks for a
                lovely day.

                (DOREEN *runs out crying.*)

GARY   (*singing*) *Dum, dum, dum, another one bites the dust. . .*

HARRY   (*to* FRANK *and* JEAN) I think that means we're leaving.

FRANK   I'll get her coat.

                (FRANK *exits very quickly.*)

HARRY   I'm sorry, Jean. I think we've got a lot of talking to do.

GARY   And we've got a lot of drinking to do.

                (GARY *disappears into the dining room to get a drink.*)

JEAN   Well, if you're sure.

HARRY   It's been lovely. Thanks for everything, Jean.

                (FRANK *enters at speed with the coat.*)

HARRY   Bye then.

                (*He kisses* JEAN *and hugs her a little too tightly. As she moves away he gooses her again.* FRANK *looks out of the window.*)

FRANK   Hey, Harry.

HARRY   What?

FRANK   Have you seen your car?

HARRY   What? (*He moves to the window.*) The little witch.

                (HARRY *grabs her coat and exits at pace.*)

FRANK   (*shouting after him*) Do you want me to plate you a dinner up for tomorrow?

                (GARY *appears out of the dining room.*)

GARY (*singing*) *Is this the real life –*
Is this just fantasy. . .

(*Music: Shakin' Stevens – 'Rock 'n Roll*
Christmas'.)

Scene Two

Early evening. JEAN *and* MILLY *sit on the sofa, dozing.*

FRANK (*to the audience*) Doreen had written all over
his car in her lipstick. I don't know how he
made it home, but, well he did. Doreen and
Harry skint. Who'd a thought it, eh? She
wouldn't wish it on anyone, but Jean was
bloody delighted. Gary, thank God, disappeared
off to Sheila's and we had the afternoon
together. Me, Jean and our Milly. Just like old
times. And Milly and Jean were talking. It was
a bit strained, but at least they were there, and
they were trying. There was one point when I
thought Jean had actually found a sense of
humour. Mothers and daughters, I'll never
understand 'em. I just kept out of the way and
let them get on with it. Well, Christmas is for
women.

MILLY Right Mam, I'm gonna have to get going.

JEAN You are going nowhere.

MILLY Mam, let's not get into –

JEAN This is your home and you're not going to
spend it somewhere else.

MILLY Mam!

JEAN I've never touched your room, it's exactly the
same as it was –

FRANK Jean! Just listen to what she's telling you.

(JEAN *is a little taken aback.*)

MILLY   I've had a great time, but, well, I've got me own
             flat now.

             (*A pause.*)

JEAN   Well, if that's what you want.

MILLY   Yeah. Yeah it is. Oh to hell with it. I wanted to
             do this today but what with Harry and Doreen
             here . . . and well I was gonna do it tomorrow
             with . . . Darren . . . but it's Christmas today
             and – oh sod it , here goes – I've got a little
             present for you.

             (JEAN *and* FRANK *exchange puzzled looks.*)

FRANK   You've already got us a present.

MILLY   That was just him showing off. No, this is from
             the both of us. And anyway it's always nice to
             have a little something to open on Christmas
             Day, isn't it.

JEAN   (*looking at* FRANK) I wouldn't know.

             (MILLY *exits.*)

FRANK   I'll get you something tomorrow.

JEAN   It's not the same.

FRANK   It'll be a surprise, though.

JEAN   I don't want a ticket for the match.

FRANK   Damn.

             (MILLY *enters.*)

MILLY   Here you go.

             (*She hands a present to* JEAN. JEAN *starts to
             very slowly and methodically unwrap it.*

FRANK, tapping his fingers, grows impatient.
He looks to the audience in disgust.
Eventually he explodes.)

FRANK   Open the bloody present. (*To the audience.*) I
         hate it when she does that.

         (*It's a very small, white, baby jacket.*)

FRANK   That'll not fit your mother.

JEAN   You mean –

         (*She looks at* MILLY, *who smiles.*)

JEAN   Oh my God!

FRANK   (*the penny drops*) Oh bloody hell. A baby. A
         bloody baby. You're gonna have a
         baby. Bugger me.

JEAN   You're only young. You've still got your life
         ahead of you. Are you getting married, is that
         the plan? I mean what're you gonna do?

MILLY   I dunno.

JEAN   But the baby –

MILLY   – will have all the love in the world.

FRANK   Too bloody right, it will. I'll kiss its bloody
         head off.

JEAN   But what about university?

FRANK   It's only a baby. Oh I see what you mean, yeah.

JEAN   I thought you were going to university next year.

MILLY   I still might.

JEAN   How the hell can you –

MILLY   Look, I haven't made up my mind. I might go
         next year or I might go in a couple of years. I'm

not gonna rush into anything. And anyway,
Darren said his mam'll look after the baby,
whatever I decide to do.

(*A pause.*)

JEAN   (*shocked*) What?

MILLY   He said, she's great with kids.

JEAN   (*defensive and hurt*) I'm great with kids.

FRANK   Oh she is.

JEAN   (*hurt*) Have you told his mam?

MILLY   No, no, we haven't told anybody. I wanted you
to be the first to know.

FRANK   I should bloody well think so, don't you, Jean?

JEAN   Listen, if anybody's gonna look after the baby
it's gonna be me.

FRANK   She's great with kids, aren't you? She went to
school with 'em.

JEAN   Right, that's settled then. (A *beat*.) Look, I just
want the best for you. I worry about you.

MILLY   I know you do. (*A beat*) Mam, I'm scared.

(*A beat.* JEAN *and* FRANK *exchange a quick
look.* JEAN *melts.*)

JEAN   Come here.

(*They embrace.*)

MILLY   (*breaking down*) Oh Mam, I'm sorry. I'm so
sorry.

JEAN   Hey, now come on. Come on.

MILLY   I've been so bloody stupid.

JEAN   Stop it. Everything's gonna be alright. Hey, come on. Come on.

                (FRANK *takes himself away, unable to deal with the emotion of it all.*)

FRANK   (*to the audience*) They're bloody soft, them two.

JEAN   Don't you worry about a thing.

                (*The girls, sensing* FRANK *is a little away, part. They turn to look at* FRANK, *who is trying to control himself.*)

MILLY   Come here, Dad.

                (FRANK, *very formally, offers to shake her hand.*)

FRANK   Congratulations.

                (MILLY *brushes past it and gives him a cuddle.*)

MILLY   Come here, you daft bugger.

                (*She throws herself on* FRANK, *who is somewhat rocked.*)

FRANK   Oh bloody hell.

                (*They embrace.*)

JEAN   Just a minute, I've got something for you.

MILLY   No, mam I don't need –

JEAN   Wait there.

                (JEAN *exits. A beat.*)

FRANK   Look, thanks for coming.

MILLY   Shurrrup. It was all down to you, you know it
          was. If you hadn't come round, well I don't
          know what would have happened.

FRANK   Yeah, well . . .

MILLY   And Mam doesn't know, does she?

FRANK   Hell no! And don't bloody tell her, for God's
          sake. Leave your mother to me, I'll deal with
          her in my own time and in my own way. (*A
          beat.*) She loves you, you know.

          (*A beat.*)

MILLY   I know.

FRANK   It's just her way. She doesn't mean anything
          by it. (*A beat.*) How's the flat?

MILLY   It's great. Dad, I'm gonna pay you back.

FRANK   Don't worry about that.

MILLY   No I am, one day. It's such a lot of money.

FRANK   It was only bloody redundancy money. Look,
          don't worry about the money, it's not
          important. But don't tell your mother I said
          that. (*A beat.*) I just want you to promise me
          one thing.

MILLY   Anything, just name it.

FRANK   If you're ever in trouble or you need anything,
          I mean anything, you come home first.

MILLY   Oh Dad!

FRANK   I mean it. This is your home. It'll always be
          your home and no matter what, that door will
          always be open for you.

(MILLY *smiles.* JEAN *enters.*)

JEAN   Here.

MILLY   Pyjamas. It's me new Pyjamas. Oh Mam!

JEAN   Look, I know it's not much.

MILLY   No, it is. It is. It's special. It was the best part
            of Christmas, getting me new pyjamas. I wanna
            put 'em on.

FRANK   Don't bloody start again, for God's sake.

MILLY   Look, I'm gonna get going. (*She struggles to
            control herself.*) Bye, Mam. Bye, Dad.

            (*A long pause. She hesitates. She doesn't want
            to go. They are all a little emotional.*)

JEAN   You're still coming round tomorrow, aren't ya?
            Both of you.

            (MILLY *smiles.*)

MILLY   Yeah, course. About eleven. Is that okay?

FRANK   You can come what the hell time you like. Your
            mother'll be up at five anyway, hoovering.

            (*A beat.*)

MILLY   Right, I'll err . . .

FRANK   Well bugger off then.

MILLY   Yeah. See you tomorrow.

            (*She holds a look before turning and exiting
            quickly.* JEAN *runs to the window to catch a
            last glimpse of her.* FRANK *goes to the front
            door to watch her up the street.*)

(*Music in: Enya – "Oíche chiúin" – "Silent Night" in Gaelic.*)

JEAN   Oh, Frank. What a bloody day.

FRANK   Yeah.

            (*They go and sit.*)

JEAN   Do you think they'll get married?

FRANK   I don't know. Maybe. Hey, they're bloody expensive, weddings.

JEAN   Oh Frank, is it important?

FRANK   You can't be going mad, Jean.

JEAN   We're not scrimping. He lives in a big house in Nunthorpe.

FRANK   Well he can pay for the bugger, then.

JEAN   Frank, they're not even getting married. Anyway we can always use your redundancy money.

            (*Unnoticed by* JEAN, FRANK *is startled and throws her a look. A pause.*)

            Can you remember when we got married?

            (*A beat.*)

FRANK   Do you know something, I never really knew what happiness was until we got married – and then it was too late.

JEAN   I was so happy. And we went to London on our honeymoon.

FRANK   Aye, we did.

JEAN   Went to Harrods.

FRANK   Spent a bloody fortune on a cup of tea.

JEAN	You know what I used to love?
FRANK	What?
JEAN	I used to love being called Mrs Bailey.
FRANK	So you should, it's quite an honour. I had plenty of women wanting that honour, don't you worry about that.
JEAN	Don't flatter yourself. It made me go all funny. I used to love writing cheques and signing them, Jean . . . Bailey.
FRANK	No change there, then.
	(*Pause.*)
JEAN	Hey, I never thought I'd end up being be married to a grandad.
FRANK	I'll be a young, trendy bloody grandad.
JEAN	(*concerned*) She's alright, isn't she? I mean we've done a good job, haven't we? I mean she's beautiful, isn't she?
FRANK	Beautiful, when she walked in, I could've bloody eaten her.
JEAN	(*smiling*) And me.
	(*Pause.*)
FRANK	Are you full?
JEAN	Stuffed. I couldn't eat another thing.
FRANK	And me.
	(*A beat.*)
FRANK	Do ya fancy a turkey sandwich?
JEAN	With stuffing.

FRANK   And a bit of cranberry.

JEAN   Aye, go on then.

FRANK   (*to the audience*) We always have turkey
                 sandwiches on Christmas night. No matter how
                 full we are, we always make room for a little
                 turkey sandwich. And you know why – 'cos we
                 can. Well it's Christmas, isn't it. Be rude not to.

GARY   (*off*) Party time!

                 (FRANK *groans.* GARY *enters through the
                 kitchen into the living room.*)

GARY   (*singing*) *All We Hear is Radio Ga Ga
                 Radio Goo Goo.
                 Radio Blah Blah
                 Radio, What's new.
                 Someone still loves you . . .*

                 There's a party at Sheila's and she wants my
                 karaoke to get the party going.

FRANK   Right, well there it is, off you go. Have a good
                 night.

JEAN   I'll show you out.

FRANK   And I'll lock the door.

GARY   You don't think I'd go without you two do
                 you? I told Sheila you were on your own and
                 she insisted you came over. Come on.

FRANK   No we can't, can we.

JEAN   No we can't.

GARY   Why not?

FRANK   (*to* JEAN) Why not?

JEAN   We're tired.

FRANK	(*feigning a yawn and a stretch*) Shattered.
JEAN	Out on our feet.
FRANK	Maybe another time.
GARY	I'm not taking no for an answer. You're not staying here on your own at Christmas. You're coming if I have to drag you there myself. It's karaoke time. And I'm gonna start off with a Christmas number. Come on, lets go. (*Singing.*) *When the snowman brings the snow,* *When the snowman brings the snow,* *He puts a great big smile on somebody's face* *Do do do do do do do do . . .*
FRANK	(*to the audience*) Oh God!
JEAN	Gary, I –
	(JEAN *tries to interrupt him on a number of occasions.*)
JEAN	Gary please, Gary. Gary, can I have a little word? Gary, just a minute.
GARY	(*singing again*) *So here it is, Merry Christmas everbody's having fun . . .*
JEAN	(*shouting to make herself heard*) Gary, shut up.
	(*Silence.* FRANK *is dumbfounded. He looks from* JEAN *to* GARY *as they exchange blows.*)
GARY	(*shocked*) What?
JEAN	And get out.
GARY	Don't you –
JEAN	Take your karaoke machine and shove it where the sun don't shine.
GARY	I'm only trying to be friend –

JEAN   Out!

GARY   Some people don't know how to enjoy
                themselves.

JEAN   (*very forceful*) Out! Now! Go on, go . . .
                (*Raising her voice.*) . . . bugger off.

                (*Frosty and Santa start dancing and singing
                simultaneously.* GARY *goes.* FRANK *looks at*
                JEAN *in pleasant wonder before running and
                locking the door behind* GARY. JEAN *sits on the
                settee.* FRANK *re-enters still smiling and still
                somewhat stunned.* FRANK *claps his hands and
                Frosty and Santa stop. Shocked, he does a
                double take. He looks to the audience, pleased
                with himself.*)

FRANK   (*to* JEAN) I've locked the door.

                (*Music in: Greg Lake – "I Believe There'll Be
                Snow This Christmas".*

JEAN   (*calm and content*) Did you say you were
                making me a turkey sandwich?

FRANK   Aye, I did.

JEAN   Lovely.

FRANK   Right.

                (FRANK *makes his way down to* JEAN *and
                speaks with tenderness.*)

                Happy Christmas, Jean.

JEAN   (*smiles*) Happy Christmas, Frank.

                (*They cuddle. Lights fade.*)